In These Quiet Moments
By Amy Jo Wrobel

TRILOGY

In These Quiet Moments

Trilogy Christian Publishers A Wholly Owned Subsidiary of Trinity Broadcasting Network

2442 Michelle Drive Tustin, CA 92780

Manufactured in the United States of America

10 9 8 7 6 5 4 3 2 1

Library of Congress Cataloging-in-Publication Data is available.

ISBN: 978-1-64773-700-9

E-ISBN: 978-1-64773-701-6

DEDICATION

Kylie and Lillie, my beautiful daughters, it's a joy and delight to be your mom. Thank you for all the material you provide by just being YOU! I love you both.

ACKNOWLEDGMENTS

My husband, Dave, my biggest fan and encouragement to follow my dreams...thank you for believing in me when I didn't believe in myself.

Kylie and Lillie, daughters and friends, you provide valuable feedback, attitude adjustments, long walks and laughter at just the right time...and sometimes ice cream!

Grant, my son in law, you ask me hard questions, giving me different perspectives as I write and are always willing to play a game and offer me encouraging hugs.

Dad (and Mom...I'm sure she's reading this from Heaven!) who gave me a solid Biblical foundation in my upbringing, answered my deep theological questions, and gave me the childhood that is shared in many of these devotionals.

My brothers, Jason and Courtney, for your invaluable input, childhood memories, and service to our country...thank you.

My sisters-in-law: Tracee, Michelle, Dana, and Shelly. I always wanted a sister and God blessed me with four beautiful godly women!

Girlfriends April, Traci, Dena, Kim, and Jolynn...you lift me up when I worry, celebrate each success, provide valuable doctrinal feedback and ideas, and accept me just as I am. Keep the "Marco's" coming!

Barb, my godly mentor for many years, not only are you the epitome of what I want to be when I grow up, you are a gifted and talented pianist. I cherish the time we spent together during the many years as the piano duo at Grace.

To my family, friends, Captain Jack, the Food Fairy, and the Keystone Church community that have prayed over me, offered ideas and opportunities to "get away from it all" so I can write without distractions, and provided me with so much material...thank you! This book is a compilation of life experiences shared with you, and you have blessed my life with your friendship.

Photography by Traci Thiele of God's Wonders Photography. Your gift of capturing God's beauty is awe-inspiring. Thank you for using your talents in this way!

Thank you seems quite insufficient, but it's deeply felt from my heart. I love you all!

CONTENTS

JOY IN CRISIS

Consider it a great joy, my brothers, whenever you experience various trials, knowing that the testing of your faith produces endurance. But endurance must do its complete work, so that you may be mature and complete, lacking nothing.

James 1:2-4

The COVID-19 pandemic is wearing me down physically, emotionally, and spiritually. Recently, I went to the store to get a few items that were needed. Normally, I only purchase what is necessary so the whole "hoarding" culture is a foreign concept to me. I tried to choose a day and time that there might be less people out and about, but also a time when the truck deliveries would have been put on the shelves.

I grabbed the few items and headed to the last aisle to grab some eggs. The entire section of eggs was bare; none were left. I've never seen this happen in my entire life. Immediately, I became irritated, and my attitude became a complaint-fest to God. So, I marched up to the checkout and informed the cashier that there were no eggs. I wasn't rude, but I wasn't pleasant either. Calmly, the cashier asked a bagger to go check in the back of the store to see if there were any eggs there. Her calming response to my heated irritation hit me like a brick. My temper melted, and I was convicted of some God truths in that moment.

In fact, it was a poignant reminder of a portion of scripture I had just taught on and am currently studying in a more "in-depth" Bible study. Even as these verses came to mind, I realized I wasn't finding joy in this trial. James, the author of the above verses, tells us we can have great joy even in the midst of trials, and, through these trials, we learn and grow in our faith to be more Christ-like. We grow in endurance and maturity, so that we will lack nothing, developed and equipped to respond well in these times of crisis.

Trials are inevitable—a normal part of life. I am often surprised by being "surprised" by the various trials and challenges I face, but according to scripture, "we will have trials." Trials are a necessary classroom in maturing a child of God because it becomes proof of one's faithful walk with God.

Let's stop and look at this little three letter word "joy." As we have been firmly enmeshed in a health crisis, we've all endured multiple trials of varying degrees. I'm sure that the situations faced are wearing thin in your own lives as well. So how can we find the great joy that James is referring to as we face various trials?

Joy is produced by the Holy Spirit as we see the beauty of Christ in the Word and in the world around us. It is a feeling of great pleasure, delighting in God as we know He is with us, carrying us through, providing for us in the trial we are walking through. Let me share with you six truths I've personally learned about joy.

1. Joy is not an emotion that can be faked. Joy is a deep-down sense of emotion in knowing our strength comes from the Lord. Nehemiah 8:10 says, "The joy of the LORD is your stronghold."

2. Joy is not dependent on our current circumstances. God continues to be our protection as we remain faithful to Him no matter what we are facing. Psalm 5:11 says, "But let all who take refuge in You rejoice; let them shout for joy forever. May You shelter them and may those who love Your name boast about You."

3. Joy is being secure in the Lord. He is our stronghold, shield, and shelter. These are military terms assuring us that God battles for us. Psalm 5:12 states, "For You, LORD, bless the righteous one; You surround him with favor like a shield."

4. Joy comes when we have an eternal view for our lives. As Christ followers, we have blessings promised to us for enduring trials and a heavenly hope that awaits us, the crown of life will be ours. James 1:12 says, "A man who endures trials is blessed, because when he passes the test he will receive the crown of life that God has promised to those who love Him."

5. Joy happens when we live in God's presence, pursuing righteous living, and valuing God's involvement in our lives. We can trust God to satisfy our needs. In Matthew 6:33 it states, "Seek first the kingdom of God and His righteousness, and all these things [*food, clothing, shelter*] will be provided for you."

6. Joy comes when we spend time praising God. Focusing on the abundant blessings benefit us and bring quiet satisfaction of knowing God continues to gift us even when we are undeserving. 1 Thessalonians 5:16-18 states, "Rejoice always! Pray Constantly. Give thanks in everything for this is God's will for you in Christ Jesus."

In humility, on my way home from the grocery store, I asked for a fresh perspective of joy in my circumstances and that it would radiate to those around me. I began to thank God for the many blessings He has been giving and doing in my life. I wasn't even done with my list of praises when I pulled into my garage. So my encouragement to you, Dear One, is to focus on the truths of finding joy in the difficulties, in the crisis, and in the mundane...and be encouraged that you too will grow and mature in Christ, reflecting His love, joy, and selflessness to the world around you, even in the challenges of trials.

Reflection

Have trials and crises made you better or bitter as you face disappointments, frustrations, trials, and challenges?

Are you allowing your emotions to control your responses?

How can focusing on joy be a life changer for you?

MAMA, WE DON'T HAVE TO WORRY

Don't worry about anything but in everything through prayer and petition with thanksgiving, let your requests be made known to God. And the peace of God which surpasses every thought, will guard your hearts and minds in Christ Jesus.

Philippians 4:6-7

Patrick, a rather tall African American youth, stood at my friend, Amber's, door one afternoon during the social distancing pandemic. Startled that someone would actually come to her door, her curiosity got the better of her and she answered. His gentle, slightly southern drawl addressed Amber regarding a community project he was involved in. His job was to deliver brochures door to door in the hopes of raising awareness and funding from the surrounding community.

As a high health risk during the COVID-19 crisis, Amber didn't take the brochure, but engaged Patrick in conversation about the project, asking who it would affect and what was needed. Suddenly, Patrick stopped the conversation and looked directly into Amber's eyes, she is also a pretty tall woman, so they met eye to eye and asked, "Mama, do you know God? I mean, do you really know Him?"

This began a deep and profound twenty five minute conversation between my godly friend, Amber, and this young man, Patrick. She affirmed that she knew God and was a Christ follower, and, having the gift of evangelism, she began to share with Patrick her testimony. Patrick began to share his new faith walk testimony, and, in a short amount of time, they were rejoicing in their common faith.

During their conversation, much to her amusement, he repeatedly referred to her as "Mama," a term she felt endearing. Amber shared honestly and transparently from her heart some of the fears she was facing in the pandemic as Patrick shared his fears about his future. Patrick then began to ask Amber hard questions, sharing that his life had not been easy, nor the choices he had made were not good choices, bearing consequences for those choices. Their hearts, knit together in the bonds of unity, went deep into the heart of the matter, and Amber offered wise counsel and encouragement to the young man.

As the conversation began to wind down, Patrick's demeanor changed to one of earnest thoughtfulness. Turning to leave, he smiled broadly at her and declared, "Mama, we don't have to worry. God said we don't have to worry." Quietly, he left, smiling a final goodbye to my friend, leaving her standing there in wonder and awe at what had just transpired on her doorstep.

You see, earlier that day, Amber had been struggling spiritually and emotionally, feeling weighed down in social isolation, acutely aware of her fragile health condition during a time of potential contamination, and feeling her relationship with the Lord was dry and arid as a desert. This unexpected visit from Patrick was a jolt to her heart that recharged and excited her. That short conversation revived her spirit and refreshed her soul.

"Mama, we don't have to worry." That audible message spoken through Patrick was the message Amber needed to hear from the Holy Spirit. It brought comfort and reassurance to her weary heart.

Jesus also reminds us in His Sermon on the Mount, Matthew 6:25, "This is why I tell you: Don't worry about your life, what you will eat or what you will drink; or about your body, what you will wear. Isn't life more than food and the body more than clothing?" If God takes care of the lesser things in life, food, clothing, and shelter, can't we trust Him to take care of the greater things of life, us? "Mama, we don't have to worry."

FLIP FLOPS AND FROGS

How happy is the man who does not follow the advice of the wicked or take the path of sinners or join a group of mockers.

Psalm 1:1

Many summers ago, I learned a very valuable lesson about fire. Enjoying a summer bonfire with my family, I stood close to the fire, enjoying the radiating heat as the sun began to set. The darker it got, the cooler the evening temperatures dropped, so I sat down in a camping chair, trying to get warm. Pretty soon, I was reclined in the chair, holding my flip-flopped feet out towards the inferno, legs propped up on an old log. As the sun began to disappear on the horizon, I got chilly and moved as close as I could to the fire. My uncle warned me not to move as close as I was, or the rubber from my flip flops would melt to my feet.

Heedless of his counsel, I continued to move even closer to the fire until I was literally a few scant inches away. Darkness had fallen, and we were getting ready to head up to the house when I stood up on my feet. It took only nanoseconds for me to realize my feet were burning...almost literally on fire! I yelped in pain and began to slide my feet through the dew drenched grass to bring cooling relief to my hot feet. As the others laughed at me for my folly, I was reminded by the croaking of the frogs that were singing by the pond that night of a story my Grandma had once told me.

You see, my Grandma was a firm believer in sharing "moral of the story" stories with my brothers and me as we were growing up. She told us the story of a frog that fell into a pot of hot water. The water in the pot was over a fire, but the frog didn't try to jump out of the pot, instead enjoyed swimming in the warm water. As the water got hotter, the frog adjusted its body temperature accordingly and continued to swim. Once the water reached the boiling point, the frog was no longer able to keep up by managing its body temperature. Eventually the frog was cooked to death. The frog couldn't make it out of the pot due to its own inability to make a wise choice on when to jump out.[1]

This "moral of the story" is just like the person of Psalm 1:1. This verse, although it starts with a positive affirmation of "how happy is the man..." actually shares three negative character descriptions. The "man" of verse one doesn't follow the advice of the wicked. I imagine him NOT hanging out at the water cooler, local hangouts, or wherever the wicked gather. Even when we just stop to "listen to the joke" or gossip, we're making a wrong choice and will be contrary to obedience to what God has told us to do.

Then I imagine the "man" not walking on the path with the sinners. Where is it that the sinners walk? Is it a specific place with a specific group of people? What are they doing? Is it good, wise, and beneficial to you? Then do not walk with them and "how happy you will be"!

But it's not enough to follow and walk with the wicked, the psalmist says, the "man" is not to join in a group of mockers. Don't take a seat and join in the raucous speech, inappropriate jokes, saying unkind or untrue things of others, or railing and mocking anyone who chooses not to join in with the worthless hypocrites and evildoers (Psalm 26:4-5).

As children of God, we all need to adjust our thinking according to the wisdom of scripture as we face different situations. In facing those situations, we should take immediate and appropriate action when we have the strength to do so before it's too late. Just like the frog, we need to be able to walk out before we need to jump.

Needless to say, I learned a very important lesson that night around the bonfire. I haven't forgotten it after all these years. Now as an adult, I see the wisdom in the benefits of following God in obedience. "Oh, how happy" expresses our joy and delight in our circumstances of being at peace in God. We can trust Him to make a way of escape when faced with "the hot water" of life.

Reflection

Have you understood the progression of sin in this way: follow, walk, and join (or perhaps your Bible translation is walk, stands, or sits)? Can you think of an instance where you fell into this trap?

Did you make the right choice in a situation that saved you from heartbreak? Thank God for helping you to be strong enough to "get out" before it was too late.

Read Proverbs 4:14-15 for further insight on staying off the path of the wicked.

THE FOUR R'S OF
SPIRITUAL WELL BEING

He gives strength to the weary; there is no limit to His understanding. Youths may faint and grow weary, and young men stumble and fall, but those who trust in the LORD will renew their strength; they will soar on wings like eagles; they will run and not grow weary; they will walk and not faint.

Isaiah 40:29-31

In our culture, we seek empowerment in our physical and nutritional goals, but we should also be seeking encouragement and empowerment in our spiritual life. Often, we give and give until we've got nothing left to give. If you don't know what I'm talking about, reflect back to a weekend or birthday celebrating you. Was it Mother's/Father's Day, a birthday, or anniversary? In some aspects, it was probably the same as other weekends. If you are like me, I'm preparing the food, cleaning up (although my husband and daughters are very helpful), and laundry still needs to be done, phone calls to make, emails to write, and text messages to respond to. We are givers by nature.

You may have a career outside the home, while others may be keepers at home. Some have small children at home, while others are empty nesters trying to figure out what to do with their extra time. Whatever position you may be in, we share a common need of spiritual, physical, and nutritional wellness.

Examine your season of life in which you are now living. Is it a balanced life? When we let our spiritual tanks run low or on empty, we are absolutely no good to anyone, even ourselves. Can you think of the last time you responded with a snarky answer, rolled your eyes out loud, or huffed and puffed at those you love? Did you even "like" you? It's so important to fill our mental and emotional tanks spiritually so that we can do the tasks that we are designed to do, whether they are raising a family, being the best spouse we can be, or fulfilling our career. If we exercise and haven't put the good nutrition into our body that is needed for the workout that we do, we don't perform as well. Our minds and hearts need the proper "nutrition" of God's Word.

So, how do we actively renew our mind, body, and spirit?

First, we need to *re-order* our lives and take inventory of what is important and prioritize. This might involve writing down a list of things that you are involved in, reviewing why you are involved in those activities, and deciding which ones are good, better, or best. Are the good activities enhancing your life? Although there may be better for you, is it the best for you?

I know personally that, several years ago, I sat down and made a list of everything I was involved in. It was draining the life out of me, and I had nothing left over for my husband and my daughters. I had to make some serious decisions and let go of some things that I enjoyed. Fearing that I was indispensable, I learned that the activity itself was dispensable. It freed up my mind and my heart and my time to concentrate on those I love the most.

Restore your body with rest, exercise, vacation, and healthy eating. Along with exercise, we know the importance of getting proper rest. Taking time away, whether to put our feet up or try to increase the number of hours we get to sleep each night is also important. Vacations are also an integral part of our better mental health and spiritual well-being. Often, being in nature, traveling, or just getting away for the day can help us refocus and clear our perspective.

One of my favorite things to do is to go hiking with my family. I tend to gravitate towards streams, rivers, lakes, and oceans. It's there that I can breathe in the life and energy of the nature that God has created. It is in those places of quiet contemplation that I can meditate on scripture that I have memorized or take time to pray. Through memorized verses and meditating on the attributes of God, it positions me in gratitude to the Creator who designed such wondrous beauty. Eating properly allows me to be in good health. Taking care of your body is vital. You are the temple of the Holy Spirit, and that reflects the outward health of the inward man. Some are naturally blessed with good health, while others struggle with health problems. However, caring for your body in whatever physical shape you are in allows you to enjoy the best of life that God has for you. In rest, exercise, vacation, and healthy eating, we have this start to physical and spiritual restoration.

Renew your mind and your spirit through times of reflection, meditation, and reading. This is something that I do each morning before my day begins. Sitting in the quiet stillness of the early morning, I spend time reading scripture and devotional books that help my thoughts align with God's thoughts. I journal life events or prayers. It's amazing how helpful journaling has been in my life. Sometimes it's good to be still and reflect on the blessings in our lives and not be consumed with the negatives in our lives.

When times are good, I spend time giving thanks, even making lists of all the things that I am grateful for. When I am experiencing difficult times, I go back and read through my journal to find encouragement and hope. I also have special verses in my Bible that are underlined for certain situations. (Personally, I encourage you to keep a set of colorful pens by your Bible to highlight or underline verses that will help you find a specific counsel or wisdom). I memorize verses by writing them on an index card and keeping them on the dashboard of my car and the mirror in my bathroom. This helps me as I go through my day, continually renewing my mind and spirit.

Reconnect with family and friends to establish meaningful relationships. We learn the importance of family when we are unable to be together, through sickness or other circumstances that keep us apart. Some of us haven't been able to be with our family in the way that we want to celebrate birthdays, anniversaries, graduations, and even funerals. However, we live in a technological age and have many ways that we can reach out and be a part of each other's lives.

Good old fashion card writing is one of the best ways to tell someone you care. I teach piano lessons and one of the ways that I stay in contact with my students is sending them cards to let them know I'm thinking about them like happy birthday wishes or a get well soon card. Recently, I received a card from one of my piano students addressed to my cats.

"Dear Major and Fancy (now that you are living with Kylie in a different city),

Meow! Hope you are doing well. I hope you two have been able to see each other on Zoom.

Stay Healthy,
Aubrey

P.S. Major, if you could, pass this along to Fancy."

It made me smile all day! Don't underestimate the importance of reconnecting in meaningful ways with special people in your life.

Trusting in the Lord will enable us to walk without fainting (endurance), run without weariness (steadfastness), soar like the eagles of the air (maturity), and renew our strength from the One who is our unlimited source of strength.

GIVE US THIS DAY OUR GLUTEN-FREE BREAD

He humbled you by letting you go hungry; then He gave you manna to eat, which you and your fathers had not known, so that you might learn that man does not live on bread alone but on every word that comes from the mouth of the LORD.

Deuteronomy 8:3

In 2014, we hosted a foreign exchange student named Nelly. She was from Eastern Europe and was such a joy and delight. In her paperwork, she had indicated a health condition that required a special diet excluding protein from her food. Nelly has a condition called PKU or phenylketonuria, a metabolic disorder leading to an increased level of phenylalanine in the blood, and, although a serious health risk, can be properly managed by diet and medication. My husband being a nurse and me being a label reader, thought we could handle Nelly's dietary issues.

That is until we realized how much fresh fruits and vegetables she required daily. Our meager food budget jumped to almost $1000+ a month to accommodate her nutritional needs. Much of the food she required were specialty items, and they cost more than "normal" foods we usually consumed. Trying to get some extra funding from the agency that sent her to us took three months of proving there was a need.

During that time, we met a doctor at a children's hospital that took great interest in our case. Since Nelly's blood needed to be regularly checked for protein levels, we got to know the doctor very well. Dr. Judy was such a blessing to us by educating us and taking care of our international student.

One day out of the blue, I received a call from Dr. Judy. A group home in a town three hours away was having to revamp their dietary requirements for a resident with PKU. As a full-grown adult, his needs had changed. They had over $1,000 worth of low/no protein food items that they were wanting to donate to a child with PKU. After some phone calls to coordinate picking up the food, the group home manager told me that many of the items had just been delivered during the past couple of days. One of the items Nelly loved was gluten free bread which wasn't often available in her country, or, if it was, it was too expensive for her family to purchase. I had been praying that God would provide bread for Nelly. And boy, did God provide!

Only God truly knew the extent of this blessing of specialty food items and bread to our family. Anyone who has a child with PKU understands the specific food requirements and how expensive these foods are to purchase. As I drove to the town to pick up the food, I was humbled that God had so abundantly answered my prayer for Nelly's "daily bread." When I got there, the bags and bags of groceries were so overwhelming that I couldn't fight the tears from spilling over.

Provisions delivered and put away in the pantry, freezer, and refrigerator created a Christmas-like atmosphere as Nelly jumped with glee at all her goodies. One of the first meals I made her was homemade tomato soup (from the abundance of tomatoes in my garden) and a grilled cheese sandwich (all with PKU-friendly food products). She had never experienced a grilled cheese sandwich before and was so excited to eat "her bread"!

This blessing from God as He provided our "daily bread" for Nelly will not be forgotten anytime soon. It was a miraculous provision, much like the manna God provided for the children of Israel. I'll never look at a loaf of gluten free bread the same again!

Reflection

How has God miraculously provided for you at a time when you needed it most?

Record these provisions by Deuteronomy 8:3 so that you will have it for a remembrance.

FOCUS ON THE TRUTH

Finally brothers, whatever is true, whatever is honorable, whatever is just, whatever is pure, whatever is lovely, whatever is commendable—if there is any moral excellence and if there is any praise—dwell on these things. Do what you have learned and received and heard and seen in me, and the God of peace will be with you.

Philippians 4:8-9

I couldn't believe what she said to me. Incredibly hurtful accusations that rocked my world. Reeling from the power of the spoken words, I took refuge in my comforting blanket and recliner chair. With tears running down my cheeks, I sat in the quietness of the morning dawn, reliving the confrontation, harsh words, angry tone of voice and the dissolution of a relationship. Like a whipped puppy, I curled in on myself, balancing my bible in my lap, and I read Psalm 41 as King David lamented the betrayal of those he held dear to him, his bosom friends, now enemies.

I felt his pain and bewilderment in the malicious intent of one close friend, as he experienced the abandonment and evil spoken against him in verse 9, "even my friend in whom I trusted...has raised his heel against me." My heart had been shattered in the words that were hurled against me. Falsity, lies, skewered perceptions and deceitful words. Cutting me deep, causing me to bleed silently and inwardly, down into my soul.

Unable to bring myself to go to our weekly church meeting, I called my pastor's wife, a godly woman and mentor to me. Through my tears, I poured out my grief to her, much as I had to God on several occasions since the incident. Silence followed my expulsion of hurts. Several heartbeats happened, and then she spoke quietly and with great wisdom gleaned from years of sitting at the feet of Jesus.

"Now listen," she began. "You must separate what was said from who said it." She went on. "Was there any truth in what had been spoken? Was there something you needed to confess before the Lord? Yes, the statements made were incredibly painful to hear, but on reflection, were any of the statements made correct?" Spending some moments chewing over these thoughts, God immediately brought to my mind areas I had "rationalized" were actually areas that needed to be dealt with: pride, anger, unforgiveness, and entitlement.

"You can't dismiss things out of hand, even when they don't have a platform or a good track record," she continued. Setting the person aside, was there truth that could be seen? Focus on the truth. What was the truth that was spoken? Had I misaligned my "godliness" with "manipulation"? Praying for God to give me wisdom in those moments, I understood James 1:5 in a new way, a profound way. Prayer for wisdom is vital to our earthly relationships.

"Prayer for wisdom, direction and a change of heart sets a powerful foundation and greater confidence in the Lord." Mrs. Barb said firmly. "Our human reasoning is no substitute for godly wisdom and power in these situations. It's not about us. The world doesn't revolve around us, for us. It's all about God. It always is!"

"God needs to be first, and you need to be surrendered in every part of your heart to God over your relationships, your spouse, your children, your family, your friends. It is then that the Holy Spirit will help you discern what is truth and what is falsehood." With that, she said good-bye and hung up the phone.

Carefully and painstakingly, I began to repeat the words of Paul, "whatever is true..." and began to dissect the words spoken. Were they words of truth or falsehood? It was like pulling weeds out of an overgrown garden. Just when I thought I had pulled them all, there were some more hidden under the flowers. Flowers that stood for truth, honor, justice, purity, were lovely and commendable. Weeds of half-truths (okay, lies), exaggerations, pride, anger, and selfishness were brutally yanked from my heart's garden. Pretty soon, the peace of God filled my heart, and the beauty of it took my breath away. In His healing power and His presence, the healing began with truth.

Reflection

Have you been the recipient of a painful confrontation? Was there truth in anything that was said to you?

Have you been able to separate the truths from the falsehoods?

What steps will you take to address the truths in your heart and life?

UPSIDE DOWN OR DOWNSIDE UP

The poor in spirit are blessed, for the kingdom of
heaven is theirs.
Those who mourn are blessed, for they will be comforted.
The gentle are blessed, for they will inherit the earth.
Those who hunger and thirst for righteousness are
blessed, for they will be filled.
The merciful are blessed, for they will be shown
mercy.
The pure in heart are blessed, for they will see God.
The peacemakers are blessed for they will be called
sons of God.
Those who are persecuted for righteousness are
blessed, for the kingdom of heaven is theirs.

Matthew 5:3-10

"It will all be turned upside down in eternity. Grief will turn
to joy. Heartbreak to shouts of thanksgiving. Crowns of
thorns to crowns of gold fit for a king."[2]

I read that sentence many times as it began to
sink in deeply. My life, definitely not what I imagined
it would be, had not turned out like my innocent childhood dreams. So much grief and heartbreak seeming
to compound with each passing year. Yet, it will all
change once I've entered heaven standing with my
Savior. Oh, Glory!

So many messages about the Sermon on the Mount have been preached and written about. So many wonderful promises God has made for living a life in Christ here on Earth. As a child, I was confused by how God seemingly took things and made them backwards, such as the simple to confound the wise and the poor to inherit.

The things that don't seem to matter in our culture are the things that matter most to God. Jesus, the King, Creator, Author, and Savior, a Servant? Jesus conquering death, by dying? Our good deeds that demand great suffering?

And yet, this is what the Kingdom of Heaven is all about.

The poor who cry out for God's help, who are fully dependent on Him for every need, are humble and contrite in spirit.

The brokenhearted who express sorrow over their sins and transgressions, feeling the weight of their sin, in repentance are comforted.

The gentle of spirit, meek, and patient, trust God fully, surrendering to His Authority even in the midst of confusing circumstances, will inherit great reward in the Kingdom of God.

Those who are ravenous for righteousness, hungry and thirsty for the Word of God, desiring the divine gift given by Jesus, Himself, will be filled with His Righteousness.

Those who exhibit forgiveness and compassion, actively showing mercy, will in turn receive mercy from the All Merciful God.

The authentic righteous one, the one whose transformation reflects Jesus, will behold God in all His glory in the new promise land.

The peacemaker, humbly serving, actively resolving conflicts, offering forgiveness, and loving their enemies will be reconciled to God. His sons and daughters accepted in their authenticity as children of His.

Those who have traded comfort for suffering, good deeds for great sacrifice, will be given a share in the kingdom as they follow Jesus' example as true disciples, serving the One Who Reigns, Jesus Messiah in His Kingdom.

As a Child of God, we can trade our pain for joy. There's a greater purpose than we might ever know here. We can trade our poverty for an eternal inheritance. There's a greater reward waiting for us.

It's upside down...but when God is at the center of it...it's downside up!

GARDEN GOODIES

Then Boaz said to Ruth, "Listen my daughter, don't go and gather grain in another field, and don't leave this one, but stay here close to my female servants. See which field they are harvesting and follow them. Haven't I ordered the young men not to touch you. When you are thirsty, go and drink from the jars the young men have filled...May the LORD reward you for what you have done, and may you receive a full reward from the LORD God of Israel, under whose wings you have come for refuge." "My lord," she said, "you have been so kind to me, for you have comforted and encouraged your slave, although I am not like one of your female servants."

Ruth 2:8-13

One summer, my garden failed to produce. Our house and yard were on the outskirts of town right next to a field of soybeans. When the farmer had his beans sprayed, which happened to be an extremely breezy day, the chemical that was used completely killed off my carefully planted garden, leaving my full and vibrant plants to wither, yellow, and die.

It was too late in the summer for a second planting and I was disheartened. Gardening was not only a hobby, but it was a necessity for our one-income family. All the fruits and vegetables that were harvested, were then frozen and canned for our winter month food preparation. This harvest would come from our meticulously maintained garden. I made salsa, jams and jellies, pie filling, and frozen green beans, peas, carrots and corn, as well as making dill pickles, sauerkraut, and applesauce. It was vital that my garden flourished and produced food for our family.

Sharing our dilemma with some friends from church, I lamented over the loss of produce in what was normally an abundantly full garden. One morning soon after, the sun hadn't fully emerged from its slumber, when I received a text message to go to our friend's farm and bring containers.

Waiting for us was a garden just bursting at its seams! Our friend stood by his garden gate and welcomed us into the garden with firm instructions to fill up our containers with the abundance of vegetables. With overflowing containers and grateful hearts, we spent the morning working in the garden, picking beans, peas, pulling carrots, and digging potatoes. We even weeded as a means to say thank you for the bounty we'd received.

For the next several weeks, church friends and family members would display their kindness by dropping off bags of garden goodies, which allowed me to begin filling our freezer and canning room! Once the apples were ready, we even received a large tote full of apples to make spicy applesauce, apple pie filling, and apple butter. The garden goodies given to us that summer were a humble reminder of God's gracious provision to us in a time of need.

This type of kindness and consideration reminds me of the story of Ruth in the Old Testament. Ruth and her mother-in-law, Naomi, were impoverished widows in a foreign land, destitute without any family or friends to call on for help.

As their daily food supply reached a critical low, the only thing for young Ruth to do was to go to the fields ripe with harvesting of barley and glean some of the barley that had fallen to the ground after the workers had been through to collect the grain. Ruth, it seems to me, was a woman of tenacity and determination as she spent the whole day, in the hot sun, following the workers and collecting as much grain as was possible to take home to Naomi.

But God, as is in His character to do, provided a rescuer to Ruth's plight in Boaz, a wealthy and noble landowner. He had arrived at his field to survey the work being done. Greeting his servants, he noticed this young woman working hard in the field. Boaz must have been a good employer, for he knew his workers, and immediately Ruth's presence stuck out to him. Asking others about her, he quickly learned her story. Moved by compassion, impressed with the care she was exhibiting for her mother-in-law, and admiring her work ethic (being there from early morning to late afternoon), Boaz instructed his servants to purposefully leave behind plenty of grain for this foreign woman.

Boaz's kindness did not stop there. He greeted her personally, offering a blessing that the God of Israel would reward Ruth's faithfulness to Naomi and provide shelter under "His protective wings." He further instructs her not to go to any other field except this field, where she would be offered the protection of his servants as she gleaned the barley and even cold water to drink. She didn't even have to go to the well to get it herself, for it was being provided for her.

It is encouraging to know that in our lives when things "happen" that these are not coincidences. They are a part of the integral planning of God's program for us. Often, we receive blessings, but are too busy to realize that these blessings are directly from the Hands of God Himself. How many times have we received a gift at just the right time? I can think of countless times that God has provided for a need that hadn't even been spoken out loud.

The difference between God and Boaz is that God already knows us, every detail of our lives, what we need and what we don't need. He knows best how to provide for our needs and even blesses us with abundance at times we don't expect it or when we need it most.

As you stay faithful to God, dear friend, may He richly bless you "for what you have done, and may you receive a full reward from the LORD God of Israel, under whose wings you have come for refuge."

Reflection

Have you ever been the recipient of someone's kindness and consideration? Were you a gracious receiver?

Are you faithful to God in helping to care for those in need, the less fortunate, widows and orphans spoken of in James 1:27?

Perhaps your blessing hasn't been monetary, but you've enjoyed good health, financial stability, harmony in your family, or any number of things. Journal a letter of gratitude to the LORD God of Israel for these blessings in your life.

GRATEFUL FOR GLADYS

I will give You thanks with all my heart; I will sing Your praise before the heavenly beings. I will bow down toward Your holy temple and give thanks to Your name for Your constant love and truth. You have exalted Your name and Your promise above everything else. On the day I called, You answered me; You increased strength within me.

Psalm 138:1-3

When Gladys came into my life, I wasn't looking for her. In fact, I was trying hard not to look at her. My day was not going well, nor my week, for that matter. My husband was a traveling nurse and was living in a different city two hours away from me at the time. I was having serious car problems and needed to trade in my well-loved and well used vehicle (topping the charts at 328,046 miles!) for something a little better on gas mileage and a lot less miles!

A few days prior to the day I met Gladys, I had traded in my favorite vehicle for what I thought was an upgrade. The sleek lines and gorgeous color as well as the functionality helped make my decision to purchase a truck. My husband always wanted a truck, and since I was working out of my home, it would be a practical tool to use for our needs as we worked in our large garden or cut down trees for firewood. I was looking at the outward appearance but had very little knowledge about what was under the hood. The choice made, and I drove off the lot with my new-to-me truck.

Within ten miles of leaving the dealership, the air conditioning stopped working...it was 96 degrees out that morning. I sweltered in the oppressive heat all the way home. Once home, I called the salesman back and told him the problem. Since it happened so soon after driving off the lot, he agreed to have the air conditioner fixed at no cost to me, but this was only the beginning of many more vehicle nightmares to come. A week later, dropping the kids off at the high school for practice, I was driving home only to have the truck catch on fire. Enough was enough! This outwardly beautiful truck was towed back to the dealership.

Sitting in the office waiting to look at a vehicle, there was only one that was available in my price range and qualifications (miles, safety, heated seats...I live in Iowa so these are a must in the winter!). As I glanced grumpily around, my eyes fell on this one particular vehicle. I sensed a nudge from the Holy Spirit saying, "That's the one." Immediately, I grumbled inwardly, "No! I don't want that one." The conversation with God was not edifying from my heart, but I remember thinking, "If that's the one, I'm going to call her Gladys. A cantankerous old woman type car." (Apologies to anyone named Gladys!)

Leaving the dealership, once again, driving home in the new-to-me Gladys vehicle, I felt myself grumbling and complaining to God. In His graciousness, God allowed me to fuss, fume, and ferment for the thirty-minute drive home. Once home, I began to work in my yard, and the Holy Spirit began to work in my heart. Psalm 138 began to play through my head and suddenly, convicted of the sin of ungratefulness, I began to worship God in gratefulness for His constant protection and provision in my life.

"I will give you thanks with all my heart." Thank you, Lord, that even though my husband wasn't here to help me, You protected me from the truck fire.

"I will sing Your praise before the heavenly beings." Lord, You give the gift of salvation that only those created in Your image can accept. Angels can only wonder at the grace given to me, a sinner saved by God's grace.

"I will bow down toward Your holy temple." On my hands and knees, pulling weeds in the beauty of the flower bed, I imagined the beauty of heaven, surrounded by perfection in all its glory illuminated by the Son of God.

"I will give thanks to Your name for Your constant love and truth." God's promises to surpass all I can ask or think as He gives me exactly what I need, not necessarily what I want.

"On the day I called, You answered me; You increased strength within me." As I continue to lean into Him, the Lord will continue to answer my prayers and petitions, offering strength when I grow weary and tired.

Gladys served our family well for many years. She endured hailstorms, hitting deer (two different times!), had quirks and issues that our mechanic could never figure out, but had also served as a bus for children going to church, and hauling students to multiple sporting and music events. I am grateful for the many miles put on that vehicle, because with each mile there were memories made, destinations visited, and a variety of opportunities to use her for the Lord's work.

I am indeed grateful for Gladys.

Reflection

Have you been called to make a choice or decision without the benefit of another's wisdom or knowledge? Have you prayed that God would direct your thoughts to make the right choice?

How can spending time with God help you make right choices in today's needs?

Are you always grateful for the gifts God gives you? If not, why not? Examine your heart to discover the reason. Then re-read the verses of Psalm 138 again and offer a prayer of gratefulness to the One Who Provides it all for you!

A PERFECT GIFT

What father among you, if his son asks for a fish, will give him a snake instead of a fish? Or if he asks for an egg, will give him a scorpion? If you then, who are evil, know how to give good gifts to your children, how much more will the heavenly Father give the Holy Spirit to those who ask Him?

Luke 11:11-13

Last Friday night, my husband, Dave, and I were on our way home from a cookout and bonfire with some friends from our small group. We had a lovely time just reconnecting after not being able to hang out for several months. Our friends own some beautiful timberland in southwestern Iowa. Hills, trees, fields, and livestock surround their property. Our friends brought out the 4-wheelers for us to ride around the boundaries of the rural property.

It was magical as we drove into the underbrush, discovering a hidden creek running through the land, finding where old buildings had been perfectly situated to have the best view of the landscape. Then we cooked out and enjoyed a delicious meal while watching the wildlife scampering around us and in the neighboring fields. The evening was topped off with a gigantic bonfire with s'mores. All of this underneath the clear dusk Iowa sunset and stars.

It had been a wonderful evening and time of fellowship. That is, until we were well on our way home, about 11:30 p.m. on Interstate 80 with long stretches of road where there are no towns, buildings, or houses, but lots and lots of deer! Suddenly, it sounded like a bomb went off in our vehicle and we were surrounded by smoke and two exploding airbags Gingerly limping our way to the side of the road, unable to see much of anything, trying to steer clear of traffic going highway speed, we sat stunned in disbelief that we had just had this rude and undesired ending to our day.

Our vehicle was totaled. We could tell that immediately. The damage was extensive. My vehicle! Once the highway patrol had been notified, Dave and I sat there in stunned silence. My first thoughts were, "What are we going to do? I haven't had a car payment in several years." Then I thought, "What kind of car will I get? Is it time to get something sportier or sleeker, or maybe finally get that truck?" (Remember we live in Iowa!)

Days later, we settled with the insurance company, and a new vehicle was found. But not without much agonizing on our behalf. Due to an incredibly generous gift from a dear (not deer) friend of ours, and our insurance settlement, we were able to purchase a new vehicle for the first time in our lives! It was almost too much for my heart and mind to reconcile.

Why? Well, because I've always had "hand-me-downs" and "used" things. Getting something new meant that it was just that, *new.* Not a scratch or dent on the vehicle and that new car scent. It was a heart altering way of thinking for me as I began to study this portion of scripture, being reminded that God delights in, takes great joy in, and gives the most perfect gifts.

In these verses, God reminds us that no human father who truly loves his children would be so unkind and uncaring as to give a gift of a rock, snake, or scorpion in place of the needed items. In fact, I imagine that God gives more gifts to us than what we realize: the gift of health, the gift of relationships, the gift of kindness and compassion through others, the gift of protection, and the gift of Himself in salvation, grace and mercy.

Lord, may we ever be mindful of the greatest gift You have given in the life of Your own Son. His great sacrifice was completed in an empty tomb. Thank you for the many gifts given that go unrecognized by us, Your children. Help us to be aware of our Heavenly Father's perfect gifts today and in the days to come. In recognizing our Father's gifts, may we in turn give good gifts to our children so that they would see You through our example. Amen.

ENDURANCE...YOU CAN DO IT!

Therefore, since we also have such a large cloud of witnesses surrounding us, let us lay aside every weight and the sin that so easily ensnares us. Let us run with endurance the race that lies before us, keeping our eyes on Jesus, the source and perfecter of our faith, who for the joy that lay before Him endured a cross and despised the shame and has sat down at the right hand of God's throne.

Hebrews 12:1

When our oldest daughter was in middle school, she decided that she wanted to join the track and field team. I didn't know what to expect and thought this desire would not last long. Boy, was I wrong! Not only did Kylie excel at short distances, she learned her body was designed for long distance running and that began for her a beautiful love affair for trail running.

Then, our youngest daughter decided that maybe she could run as well. Kylie spent time helping Lillie develop her technique, endurance, and stamina. Soon they were both "off and running" together. I loved watching them disappear over the horizon, running in sync with each other, while the bond of sisters deepening with their shared love of running.

Last year, my husband did something that was *huge*! He signed up to do a half-Iron Man triathlon. He began training intensely with swimming, cycling, and running. He started off slow, never really having been a triathlete. When they were available, the girls would run with him, and I would hear them say, "You can do it, Dad! You can do it!" Gradually, he built up his endurance, strength, and stamina by running slowly at first, but running steadily.

In attending track meets and practices, I've noticed that often friends or family members who are cheering on their athletes will start moving with those in the race, supporting them, encouraging them, and even running alongside them as they race towards the finish line. It's a profoundly moving thing to watch, even more so when I watch my girls cheer on their dad.

I've seen dads run alongside their children who were struggling in a race. I've seen siblings join in the race to help when a side stitch has disabled a brother or sister. I've seen coaches run across the field to pick up a runner who is injured. I've seen teammates who double back to run with a slower runner.

As Jesus Followers, shouldn't we be emulating this same kind of support and encouragement with our brothers and sisters? I'm frequently convicted by my lack of encouragement to a sister who is weighed down by the bad choices she's made or a brother who has fallen by the side. Just like the teammates who double back, I should be running back to run beside those who don't yet have the strength and endurance in running this race.

The writer of Hebrews was writing to people who understood the depth of meaning in these verses. Greek and Roman athletes would vie for a position at representing their countries and communities well. It was a patriotic privilege to be a good athlete and bring prestige and glory to the country they represented.

Just like the athletes spoken of, some of us grow weary and faint, and others press on for the prize, running the race with endurance (Isaiah 40:31; Philippians 4:13; Hebrews 12:1-2). This endurance also means "patience," "steadfastness," and "fortitude." Running a race requires discipline of diet, physical training, and mental preparation.

As Christians, our earthly race requires physical discipline, "laying aside every sinful weight and sin that so easily ensnares us." Our disbelief, lies of this world, and apathy. It requires the mental discipline of endurance, "Let us run with endurance the race set before us." This same endurance is spoken of in James 1:2-4. Finally, the Christian race requires spiritual discipline as we "keep our eyes fixed on Jesus as the author and finisher of our faith" (Hebrews 12:2). Jesus not only ran the race, but He finished the work the Father gave Him to do, suffering for the sins of all the world, now sitting at the right hand of the throne of God because His work is completed (John 17:4; Hebrews 12:2). His race is won.

So, as you continue to run this race, know that you have the ability to endure—"You can do all things through Christ!" (Philippians 4:13).

Reflection

Is there a particular race you are running? Are you weary?

Where is your strength and endurance coming from?

Have you been caring for your physical, emotional and spiritual needs as you run the race as a Christ follower? What changes do you need to make to continue to run with endurance?

I CAN'T CATCH A BREAK

Five times I received 39 lashes with rods by the Romans. Once I was stoned by my enemies. Three times I was shipwrecked. I have spent a night and a day in the open sea. On frequent journeys, I faced dangers from rivers, dangers from robbers, dangers from my own people, dangers from the Gentiles, dangers in the city, dangers in the open country, dangers on the sea, and dangers among false brothers; labor and hardship, many nights hunger and thirst, often without food, cold and lacked clothing...

2 Corinthians 11:24-27

I feel like my family's motto should be, "If it's going to happen, it will happen to us!" This past winter, it seemed like we had more of these days than we had good days. The pipes froze in polar vortex chills of the Iowa winter climate. My vehicle had some problems. Our youngest daughter had some health issues. Money was going out faster than it was coming in. My husband was working so much overtime due to the surgery demand at the end of year that he got into trouble (of no fault of his own) with upper management. My piano studio was experiencing growing pains, and I was thoroughly exhausted. The stressors of life were gnawing away at our peaceful home where critical speech and impatience seemed to have taken over. Not to mention all of the things going on in our extended family and church life. It was all just too much. I couldn't catch a break!

So, I stopped and opened my Bible. God led me to a portion of scripture where it seemed like the Apostle Paul just couldn't catch a break either. As I began to read what Paul endured, my challenges and irritations began to melt away as I realized I was in good company. If the Apostle Paul couldn't catch a break, then I'm honored to be in the same "boat" as him.

Then I realized why he was relating his suffering to those he was speaking to. Paul was exasperated with the immaturity and lack of spirituality of the Corinthians that began to question and contend with him, seemingly to be constantly defending his position in Christ. As I dug deeper into the many hardships and suffering of Paul, the one thing that stood out to me is his love for Christ and his wanting to glorify Him in serving and evangelizing even when things didn't go his way, or when he didn't have enough food, water, or sufficient clothing to take care of his personal needs.

Not only did Paul humble himself in these ways for the glory of God, but also because of his profound love for the young believers who had not yet grown enough in their spiritual life to recognize the difference between the false teachers and Paul's testimony of truth in Christ. Which is why he began this diatribe of "boastings" to counter the boastings of the false leaders. Paul's boasting reminds me of Proverbs 26:5, "Answer a fool according to his foolishness or he'll become wise in his own eyes." He was making a point that these false leaders were not ashamed to boast, so Paul responded in kind.

As I thought about the hardships that I had been going through, God seemed to nudge my heart to point out my ingratitude and selfish attitude towards Him, where the Apostle Paul, often humiliated and abused, was willing to do so for the cause of Christ. Perhaps, God seemed to say, this is why I trust you with these burdens, sufferings, and hardships, because you will glorify Me in your response and testimony. Quietly, I prayed for forgiveness of the ways I have failed Him in these moments and asked for strength to continue to endure for the cause of Christ.

A servant's heart full of humility
May others see Christ in me
Not just the sufferings I endure
But a life lived for God that is pure

Dangers, struggles, hardships, too
Not just a hearer but one that will do
Carry the gospel to those in need
Proving my love for the church indeed

In hardship, sleeplessness, hunger and thirst
May I put my Lord God above all first
That He would use the weak in me
To exalt Himself and receive the glory

ON YOUR LEFT

Carefully consider the path for your feet, and all your ways will be established. Don't turn to the right or to the left; keep your feet away from evil.

Proverbs 4:26-27

In the last few years, our family has become avid bike riders and love riding the many trails that are in our area. Our favorite trail is the High Trestle Trail. The High Trestle Trail runs for twenty-five miles through five towns and four counties and includes the iconic half mile thirteen-story high bridge across the Des Moines River Valley. This was one of the most complicated trail projects in Iowa. It covers some of the most picturesque landscape this river valley has to offer, even being able to see the downtown Des Moines high rise buildings when the atmosphere is clear.

However, in my education of riding trails, I have become familiar with a phrase that is important to remember to use while cycling. This trail is not only a cycling trail, but a hiking trail, and on beautiful Iowa days, it can have a high traffic volume. So it's important to make others aware of your position: "*On your left*" designates your course of action so that a walker isn't hit or a cyclist isn't forced off the trail onto loose gravel, large rocks, or sometimes even down steep ditches that line the trails.

Early on in my cycling hobby, I used to be shy and not cry out, "On your left," leaving that to my husband or daughters to do. But on one occasion, I was just enough behind my husband that a group of walkers thought Dave was alone and began to spread across the trail again. It was almost the cause of a serious accident. All because I didn't "carefully consider my path" and call out to the walkers, and because the walkers were too busy joking around to pay attention to others on the trail.

In Proverbs, we have such great wisdom and guidance that to ignore these important chapters would label us "fools," and the idea that we find in the above verses is that God promises to direct our path and protect and perfect our way along the path as long as we walk in the way of His Wisdom (Proverbs 1:7). I've noticed that when walking on trails (or even in my yard) when lighting is limited, like dusk or early morning hours, that I tend to be more cautious and watch my footing more carefully. I've stepped into hidden holes and broken my foot a couple of times. I'm more aware now of where my feet are walking.

As we walk one of two paths here on Earth, the narrow path and the wide path, we need to pay close undivided attention to the narrow or right path (Matthew 7:13-14). As we do, God will establish our way, keeping our feet away from evil. If we choose the wide path, or the way of folly, it will lead us into danger, disappointments, and, ultimately, death.

Depending on your Bible translation, verse 26 starts with a suggestion to "carefully" (in a way that deliberately avoids harm or errors), or "ponder" (to weigh, make level, or balance) the path before us. May we be like the son in Proverbs, wisely choosing to listen to his father, by paying close attention to the godly counsel given to us in these verses and not swerving, but staying the course allowing God to guide our steps.

Reflection

Have you been "careful" to consider the path you are on?

Are you on the narrow path, which symbolizes the path that leads to Christ's Kingdom (2 Corinthians 13:5)? Or are you lost on the wide path of destruction?

Call out to Jesus to guide your path. He promises to establish your way when you walk in His Wisdom and Love.

WE DON'T CHOOSE THE HARD: PART I

> Now we have this treasure in clay jars, so that this extraordinary power may be from God and not from us. We are pressured in every way but not crushed; we are perplexed but not in despair; we are persecuted by not abandoned; we are struck down but not destroyed. We always carry the death of Jesus in our body, so that the life of Jesus may also be revealed in our body...Therefore we do not give up. Even though our outer person is being destroyed, our inner person is being renewed day by day.
>
> 2 Corinthians 4:7-10, 16

I have many different types of vases. I love cut flowers, and, when I used to have a much larger flower garden, I would place bunches of flowers all over my house as well as give flowers to family and friends. Some of the vases are inexpensive. I've even been known to use old canning jars or jam jars to hold the many flowers from my gardens.

I also have some precious and decorative vases. I don't use them very often because they are more fragile and expensive, and some are heirlooms. The cut glass designs are intricate and beautiful. The etchings are detailed and painstakingly created.

When one of my cheap vases breaks, I'm not too concerned; instead, I am more annoyed at the mess I have to clean up. But, if one of my treasured vases gets a crack in it or shatters, I get very upset knowing that it is irreplaceable because of the lineage and stories that accompany the vases I've inherited. I can't get them back nor can I find exact replicas, or, if I can find replicas, they are too expensive for me to replace.

What I often forget about all of the containers, is that they are just that—containers. It's not what they are that is important, but what they contain. The vases are made more lovely by what they hold: beautiful flowers.

Clay jars represent for us a metaphor of the human body, which is fragile and mortal. Isaiah 64:8 reveals to us that it is God our creator that shapes and designs us as the artist or potter of the clay. But notice in these verses that it's not the physical appearance or "clay jars" that bear the beauty, but what is inside the clay jars.

Treasure is in these clay jars. What kind of treasure? Well, it's the treasure of the unfading glory of Jesus Christ. As we accept Him as Lord of our lives, we invite Him to work a powerful work in us through the gift of the Holy Spirit. He's our treasure, a priceless treasure that was bought with the blood of Jesus Christ to purchase us. We frail fallible human beings bear the scar of sin and are made beautiful, purchased with the treasure of God in the form of His Son, Jesus.

As is often the case with paradoxes of many Biblical teachings, contrary to what we view as beautiful and priceless in material possessions, God counts beautiful in the more humble looking of containers in humans. What is more humble on the inside is more glorious because it allows the preciousness of the content to appear more brilliantly. God doesn't look on the outward appearance, but on the heart of man (I Samuel 16:7).

I have a dear friend named Teri. Even as I write this, she is experiencing difficulties and challenges that are stretching her very thin right now. We speak frequently, pray for each other, and lift each other up as we continue to walk this journey of life together as friends. What she doesn't see is how beautifully Christ is being reflected through her during this time enduring the "pressure" of her trials. The "treasure" in her is shining brilliantly through her humility as a servant of her Lord and Savior.

Another friend deals with health issues but refuses to allow her health to hinder her from sharing the love of Jesus with every person she comes into contact with, even when it could jeopardize her precarious health. Her humble "container" of clay is magnified by the beauty that radiates from the power she possesses in Jesus Christ.

Rachael is one of those "God moment" friends, brought together through a set of circumstances several years ago, only to have our friendship blossom during a time of deep pain for her. Her quiet and kind demeanor hides a heart that has been broken and rejected, yet her life yields the beauty and glory of a redeemed woman carrying the beauty of her Savior. Her humility is awe-inspiring, yet she would only shake her head and deflect the glory to her Refuge and Strength, her Jehovah-Jireh.

Friend, I want you to see yourself as God sees you in this moment.: His fragile jar of clay, treasured because of what you possess, His Son, Jesus Christ. Because of this treasure you possess, God has set you apart, sanctified you to be prepared and used, available for His service. It is in our suffering that God allows some of the treasure to spill out so that others might see and believe and have hope.

May God be glorified in these jars of clay.

WE DON'T CHOOSE THE HARD: PART 2

> Now we have this treasure in clay jars, so that this extraordinary power may be from God and not from us. We are pressured in every way but not crushed; we are perplexed but not in despair; we are persecuted by not abandoned; we are struck down but not destroyed. We always carry the death of Jesus in our body, so that the life of Jesus may also be revealed in our body...Therefore we do not give up. Even though our outer person is being destroyed, our inner person is being renewed day by day.
>
> 2 Corinthians 4:7-10, 16

We learned previously that it's not in ourselves that we are worth anything, but the treasure that resides in us. However, what happens when hard things happen, when we endure pressure and challenges, sickness, fear, financial ruin, rebellious children, marital problems, or death? How can these tragedies be beautiful? Why does God allow us to experience difficult circumstances and trials?

How best can we identify with the sufferings of Christ, but to go through sufferings and trials? We walk with Him, bearing His image, sharing in His testimony and His glory. It is in times of learning, growing, and suffering that we become more Christlike, able to more effectively communicate the gospel of Christ.

Dr. John Henry Jowett said, "Ministry that costs nothing, accomplishes nothing." He was right. A pastor friend and I once heard a young man preach an eloquent sermon, but it lacked something. "There was something missing," I said to my friend; and he replied, "Yes, and it won't be there until his heart is broken. After he has suffered awhile, he will have a message worth listening to."[3]

In these verses, the Apostle Paul is encouraging the believer that we are going to experience hardships of various kinds, just as James 1:2-4 teaches. It is through these difficulties that God's power is evident in the life of a faithful believer. Paul was confident that his life was being lived to its fullest, representing the message of victory in Christ. Christ suffered; therefore, it is only natural that, as His followers, we will suffer.

Some suffer from the consequences of poor choices. However, as we remain usable vessels set apart for God's will and purpose, we have the assurance that God will be glorified in our suffering. We can endure in steadfastness, not giving up, but experiencing victory in Jesus Christ and the promise of rewards to come (James 1:12).

In the arrogance of my youth, I was often critical of my parents and the decisions they made during times of trials. I thought I could make better choices, wouldn't react certain ways, and, ultimately, I would be a better Christian. It wasn't until the reality of marriage, disappointment and hurt, financial challenges, and the death of a child humbled me so completely that

I recognized that my parents had attempted to use their trials and sufferings to bring glory to God. When I humbled myself as an empty broken vessel to God, He filled me with His treasure and power, and it allowed His glory to shine through me.

This was evident after our daughter, Ellie, died. Dave and I were only twenty six years old when I gave birth to our stillborn daughter. I struggled to understand how God could use something so devastating in our lives for anything good. But in only a few short months, God would reveal to us how we would be able to minister to others who had endured the death of an infant.

A dear couple in our Sunday school class, Stephen and Mary, were pregnant with twins and had just been admitted to the hospital. Mary was in labor prematurely. I don't remember all the details of this difficult time, but I do remember receiving a phone call from Mary's mother asking me to come visit Mary in the hospital. One of the twins didn't survive. Mary wanted me to come see her because I knew what it was like to experience a stillborn. She needed the comfort and encouragement of someone who had walked that path before her.

Frequently, the trials we've been given to endure are to help others walking similar paths, offering hope to the weary and worn, bringing encouragement to the down trodden. In it all, the trials reflect the treasure and power of Christ in our lives so that others will see His glory.

Paul ends these verses reminding us that, as he experiences trials and hardships, they are working for his good, to make him a better servant of Christ. Paul's spirit of faith encourages us to grow spiritually as children of God so that God is glorified through our lives here on Earth. Even when our bodies are beginning to fade from weariness, sickness, or trials, our inner man can be renewed daily. We can gain for each day the grace needed for that day, sufficient to rest in God's care and provision for each trial that comes our way (Hebrews 4:16).

Reflection

Dear friend, are you being pressed in on every side? Come to the throne of grace with boldness. Share your trials with the Lord. Ask for grace to help you at the proper time. Write your prayer here...

START AT THE END

Look! I am coming quickly, and My reward is with Me to repay each person according to what he has done. I am the Alpha and the Omega, the First and the Last, the Beginning and the End.

Revelation 22:12-13

My dad once said to me, "If I had known being a grandparent was going to be like this, I would have skipped having kids and gone directly to being a grandparent." I pretended to be offended but laughed instead as I observed the joy radiating from his face as he was surrounded by his grandchildren.

At one time, there were only four grandchildren, born all within three years of each other. Several years later, there was another one added, and even more years later there were two more added. His joy and delight in his grandchildren haven't diminished as struggles with Parkinson's and dementia. He continues to pray for each of his grandchildren. His fireplace mantel is filled with pictures of each one, large enough he can gaze on them from across the room even with failing eyes.

I wonder how many of us would start projects or jobs if we really could fathom the end result at the beginning. When we built our house, it was difficult for me to visualize the end result of the beautiful modern Victorian house that was being built. I grew impatient and restless as days turned into weeks and weeks into months, when finally we were able to move in and start making the house our home. It was then, at its completion, that I finally saw the project that we had dreamed of for many years in finality.

As parents of newborns, we can't see past the seemingly endless nights of a crying baby, a potty-training toddler, or the challenges the teen years bring.

When one graduates from college, they are in the infatuation stages of their first "real" job, often not even thinking of the weight of all they will do in the intervening years up to retirement. Investing not only in their retirement fund but investing in their development and growth to become who they desire to be and earn the income they desire for the here and now, perhaps with the future in mind, but perhaps not.

Walking down the aisle, deeply in love with the man or woman of their dreams, the fulfillment of the greatest bond as husband and wife, thoughts aren't on the final years of aging or the physical and mental deterioration, such as nursing a spouse through the challenges of ALS, Alzheimer, or cancer.

I often wonder how much differently we would live our lives if we focused on the End. How many of us would live more intentionally? Would we work harder and invest more? Would we pray differently or pray more fervently? Is it possible that our lives would be more fulfilling and meaningful with the End in view as we started at the beginning?

I have to admit that as a child, I had a bad habit when I started a book, if it happened to be "slow going" at the beginning, I would jump to the end and read the last chapter. If it was an exciting ending, I would go back to the beginning and start reading again. If the ending was a dud, I stopped reading the book. Occasionally, as I got older, I'd go back and pick up the book and try again. Sometimes, I found that my maturity allowed a new and fresh perspective on the book, and I would be intrigued to finish what I had previously started.

As I read these verses in Revelation, my imagination runs wild with all the descriptive verses John gives us of the New Heaven and the New Earth. As the book of Revelation winds down in Chapter 22, I'm aware of a quickening in my heart knowing that soon I will be personally walking these streets of gold, walking along the river of living water, fixing my eyes on the throne of God and of the Lamb, serving the Lamb who illuminates the city just by His presence.

However, the thing that sticks out the most to me in the verses above is that Jesus contrasted the "beginning and the end" by referring to Himself. The Creator, Author of the world, who began before the world was even created had the End in sight before He even began. And at the time of John's recording of Jesus' words, Jesus was already contemplating His return, and it was to be "quickly."

He is the Alpha and Omega. The first and last letters of the Greek alphabet, like "A to Z" in the English language. He is the First and Last. The Author and Finisher of our faith. He is the Beginning and the End. The work of judgment and redemptive work completed on the cross by the Lamb of God.

In concepts too much for our finite brains to comprehend, as the Christian gospel song goes, "When He was on the Cross, I was on His mind." Jesus Christ began at the beginning of time with thoughts of you and me, already with Him in eternity to come in the New Heaven and New Earth. Participating in His glory as His redeemed creation, enjoying all things He prepared "aforetime" for us, and He's ready for us.

Not only did Jesus start at the End, He is going to reward us each individually, repaying us according to the works we have done for HIs Kingdom. It reminds me of a "retirement package" that Jesus has set in place for us as we serve Him in this life. We have the promise of eternal life with Christ when we seek to follow and love Him, but He will also reward us for doing so.

Reflection

How about you dear friend? Have you started your walk with Christ starting with the end?

How would you live your life differently if you understood the abundant blessings waiting for you as you serve the Lord with your life? You can start afresh today...start with the end in mind!

WHAT TEMPERATURE ARE YOU?

"The Amen, the faithful and true Witness, the Originator of God's creation says: I know your works, that you are neither cold nor hot. I wish that you were cold or hot. So, because you are lukewarm and neither hot nor cold, I am going to vomit you out of My mouth."

Revelation 3:14-16

Iowa is hot, humid in the summer and cold, windy in the winter. We experience varying degrees of temperature, often within the same day. It has been said, "If you start out the day with a sweatshirt and change several times in the day, you might be in Iowa." I love the weather diversity that surrounds each of the seasons here. When it's hot...it's hot. When it's cold...it's cold. When it's humid...it's corn season!

Going cycling with my husband, I have learned to take a water bottle filled with ice and then cold water. Not long into our summertime bike rides, I found I needed more water as I got hotter and was using more energy to pedal. I tried to drink sparingly so that I had water for the return trip, but the ice had melted and the water had become warm, almost undrinkable. After doing this several times, I now prepare extra bottles of cold water to have on hand at the end of our bike rides.

I also enjoy a piping hot cup of coffee in the late autumn weeks when the weather is crisp and cool, a precursor to the winter snow. Sitting on my deck enjoying my "alone time with God," if I don't drink my coffee right away, it will cool too quickly and end up undrinkable. In either case, the drink that was cold turned hot, and the hot drink turned lukewarm, neither providing the quenching I desired.

When I read these verses in Revelation about the church at Laodicea, I'm reminded of these two different thirst-quenching drinks. I can't think of anything that satisfies that is a lukewarm temperature. That's why the word picture that God describes here really made sense to the church in Laodicea. You see, the church in Laodicea was in the center of two locations that piped in water...cold refreshing water from Colossae, which was ten miles south, and the hot therapeutic spring water was piped in from Hierapolis, which was seven miles north of Laodicea. The water would arrive in Laodicea as lukewarm water, ineffective and useless, not satisfying the need for ice cold water or hot spring water.

Jesus was nauseated by the church's behavior in Laodicea, so much so that He was ready to vomit them out of His mouth with their worthlessness and apathy. It seems very harsh to hear these words, but the truth is that they were not palatable to the Lord or the people in their community. With the three degrees of water, I often wonder what I am as a follower of Christ and what the world-wide church is as the bride of Christ.

What does a cold church or follower of Christ look like? Perhaps It is the relationship that has grown "cold," rigid with formality and legalism, active in opposition to the gospel because it's more important to follow the law of the Old Testament rather than living out the law of liberty and grace. In the windy cold Iowa winter, you can find me wrapped up in a warm fuzzy blanket because the coldness of the wind literally takes all my energy away, leaving me lethargic and shivering. I wonder if this is what Jesus was referring to.

But what about the hot church or follower of Christ? What does this look like? Is your life full of zeal and passion for Christ? Are you on fire for the things of Jesus? Does spiritual excitement grip you when lives are changed for Christ? When you see the redemption of a lost soul? The beauty of the baptism of one who is declaring publicly their desire to follow the Lord? Is your love for Christ igniting the world around you? I see this kind of "hot," on fire for Jesus temperature on videos of unreached people groups hearing about the love of Jesus Christ for the first time. Or Bibles being printed in obscure languages given to people who have never read the Bible in their own language before. This kind of "hot" sets the heart on fire with love for the Savior and Redeemer that purchased a wayward people from the condemnation of sin.

So, what happens when one grows lukewarm? Does a lukewarm church that ceases to be on fire for the Lord become ineffective? Can you think of anything pleasant about a lukewarm shower or bath?

How about a lukewarm sink of sudsy water trying to wash a greasy pan? Would you enjoy a specially prepared lukewarm dinner? Or a cup of lukewarm coffee or a glass of water? There is nothing very satisfying in these examples of a lukewarm nature.

What is your temperature? Are you cold and constricted in your love for the Lord? Or do others see your passion in sharing the gospel to the world around you on fire for Jesus? Maybe you are lukewarm in your attitude towards the things of Christ? I encourage you to "turn up the heat" and stop going through the motions of playing Christian.

Reflection

Do your speech and behavior represent hot, cold or lukewarm temperatures spoken about in Revelation 3:14-16? How is this a God-honoring temperature?

What can you do to change the temperature of your speech or behavior?

How could changing the temperature of your spiritual life assist you with the temperature of your words?

LITTLE FOXES

Catch the foxes for us—the little foxes that ruin the vineyards—for our vineyards are in bloom.

Song of Solomon 2:15

There was a young couple who were deeply in love. They would walk hand in hand and dream of their future lives together. One day, they were married and began to build a home, just the two of them. The young woman had grown up with parents who left each other little unspoken messages throughout the day to let the other know that they were thinking of them and praying for them. The young man grew up watching his parents outwardly displaying passive aggressive tendencies, but secretly criticized and complained to others of their spouse.

In the early months of their lives, she would let her husband know that she cared deeply for him, loved him, and prayed for him by neatly folding his laundry, praying that God would continue to mold him into the man of God that she knew he was capable of becoming. When she prepared his meals for when he arrived home each night, she thanked God for the food that her husband's job paid for and that her husband came home to her each night to her so they could enjoy the meal she prepared for him together. She left him messages written on the bathroom mirror or tucked love notes into his lunch bag.

In much the same way, the husband would often notice little things around the house and yard that could be done that would allow him to show his young wife just how much he cared for her. As he broke down boxes and put them in the recycling bin, took the trash out, and did garage maintenance, he thanked God for blessing him with a job that provided them with the little extras of ordering special things for the house that came in the boxes he was tearing down. He thanked God for all the tools that hung in the garage that he used to plant the garden, do yard maintenance, and, in the winter, snow removal, all the while, praying for his wife. Grateful, he thanked God that his wife was talented in making little look like much, turning their living space into a real home.

Over the years, the messages started fading away. Irritated with the amount of laundry, the number of boxes, and the general stresses of life, they each began to silently grumble their complaints to the Lord. They began to bicker and quarrel with each other. The unspoken language was turning to one of resentment and dislike, dissatisfaction and annoyance. The love that once burned hot and warmed them through the coldness of difficulties and challenges had lost its fervor.

The sad truth was they were allowing those silent messages of love and caring turn into aggravation.

Even though they still loved each other, the love they once shared was fading away.

One day, it surprised the man to see there were no more messages. The man looked around and realized his wife was no longer there. No one to fold his clothes, no one to make his meals, and just as poignantly, he noticed there were no more boxes to be broken down in the garage. There was no garden planted in the yard, and he hadn't been puttering around much in the garage. His heart grew very sad. He understood then how much she was saying she loved him, and he didn't even realize it.

The little foxes spoken of in the above verse are harmful. They get into the vineyards and wreak havoc on the grapes that weigh down the grapevines. Farmers must be ever vigilant against the destruction of these little creatures.

The little foxes can get anywhere in our lives, quietly destroy relationships whether with our spouse, our children, our families, or our friends. We must be ever aware not to allow the beauty of our marriages, parenthood, friendships, or other relationships to become harmed by life's irritations, contempt, misunderstandings, and pride. We must tend our garden carefully, just as the keepers had to tend their grapes.

Reflection

Have you allowed "little foxes" to creep into your marriage? What could you do to repair the damage done?

How can you bring back the beauty of romance to your marriage?

Write down some ways that you can show your spouse, a child, or a friend that you love them...then pick one each day and do it...and repeat!

MULBERRY STAINS AND
A WHITE COWBOY HAT

Come, let us discuss this, says the LORD. Though your sins are like scarlet, they will be as white as snow; though they are as red as crimson, they will be like wool. If you are willing and obedient, you will eat the good things of the land...

Isaiah 1:18-19

Growing up in rural Iowa, my favorite thing to do in the summer was spend time on my grandparent's farm. Grandpa and Grandma were as different as night and day. Where he was tall and lithe, she was short and stout. Where he was stern and gruff, she was indulgent and permissive. He loved his horses, and she loved her cats.

It was always an adventure spending time on their farm. There were forty acres of adventurous experiences for a child to have. There was a grove of trees that had great climbing trees, paths and trails that wound around the extent of the farm, horses to ride, berries to pick, and barns full of all kinds of mischievous potential. Grandpa and Grandma had a lot of Old West reenactment clothing that they would wear as they drove their teams of horses for parades, weddings, family gatherings, but the biggest event ever was the '76 Bicentennial Wagon Train as they drove a team of horses in a covered wagon from Iowa to Valley Forge, Pennsylvania.

Grandpa had a special white felt cowboy hat he wore. Grandma's bonnet was handmade and lined with ruffles, tying under her chin. On the Wagon Train, they were decked out in their finest "period piece" clothing. After it was all over, we grandchildren were allowed to play dress up with their reenactment clothes, and we loved it! We would sit in the wagon all dressed in their clothes, pretending to drive horses over the rutted trails headed out west.

One summer, I was old enough to go pick mulberries and bring back enough for pie. We were once again dressed up, and my brothers and I headed out to the old windmill to pick mulberries. Once we got there, we realized we hadn't taken our bucket with us. I was wearing Grandpa's white felt cowboy hat with white satin lining and thought it would be a good idea to put the mulberries into the hat and carry them back. After all, they were just "play clothes," and Grandma was looking forward to baking that mulberry pie. Needless to say, when Grandpa saw his berry-stained hat, I thought it best to "skedaddle" a bit and let him cool off. I can still hear Grandma's voice saying, "Now Clyde, she's only a child."

That stained white cowboy hat has haunted me all these years. You see, I'm not sure I ever had a chance to apologize to my Grandpa since he died shortly after that summer. It hurt to think that my choice caused such damage to something he loved. His hat was never the same.

Reading these verses, I'm reminded of another kind of stain. The stain of sin. Its color is scarlet. In the preceding verses here in Isaiah 1, the prophet had been describing a courtroom scene with God as the judge and the nation of Israel as the defendant. Declared guilty before a righteous judge, Israel's sins and rebellion had broken the covenant that God had established with Israel (Exodus 19-20).

Guilty of many sins, the most abhorrent to God is their idolatrous adultery. Their "religion" was hypocritical and "their hands were stained with blood" from their many sins. Isaiah was laying out God's case against this faithless nation, much as a lawyer lays out a case before a judge. But Isaiah did not stop here.

He didn't want them to just realize their sins. He wanted to offer a solution through repentance to the One True God. "Reason" in verse 18 translates to "to decide a case in court," but the Judge here is not issuing a judgment and penalty, but hope and pardon by cleansing their hearts as they express true repentance. Their sins that were scarlet would be made to be as white as snow.

God offers us this opportunity to turn from our sins and follow hard after Christ through the one-time sacrifice of His only Son on the cross. The blood that ran freely that day, washes your sins and mine white as snow, forgiven for all eternity. The gift offered is free. It's up to you to accept the gift of redemption.

After that incident with the mulberries and Grandpa's white felt cowboy hat, I felt like God was giving me a personalized example, so that every time I think of those stains, I think of my sin. Years later, I was helping to clear my grandparent's house to put it on the market to sell. I came across the hat setting in an old hat box in Grandpa's closet.

The stains were a faint memory. Grandma had worked hard on removing the mulberry juice stains, but there they were, a faded memory. No amount of cleaning with detergents could get the stains completely out. I wasn't able to make things right with my Grandpa. I didn't have an opportunity to ask for forgiveness.

But God tells us that when we repent, our sins are immediately changed to white. Forever white. In a state of being cleansed and having been cleansed. Forgiven. God has every right to punish us because of our sin, just as He had every reason to punish the nation of Israel. In His lovingkindness, His grace and mercy offered to us, He chose instead to offer us pardon.

God will wipe our record clean. No more stains. White as snow.

DANGER! DANGER!
YOUR TONGUE'S ON FIRE!

So too, though the tongue is a small part of the body, it boasts great things. Consider how large a forest a small fire ignites. And the tongue is a fire. The tongue, a world of unrighteousness is placed among the parts of our bodies. It pollutes the whole body, sets the course of life on fire, and is set on fire by hell.

James 3:5-6

A few years ago, I was the recipient of some damaging gossip that ran rampant through a group of people. When I was able to get to the bottom of the unjust and unfounded accusations, one single person was the culprit. This person's jealousy over my position of leadership fanned the flames of slander and character defamation. I was personally devastated.

My husband tried to console me that those who really knew me would know the truth and not believe the lies. But my character and judgment had been called into question and the damage had been done. Not only had verbal arrows been fired, they left their damage in my heart, and I was wounded.

Recently, I was told about a scandalous affair regarding a couple that had come to mean a great deal to my husband and myself. As I listened to what was being said,

I was reminded of these verses. Once the speaker had finished, I remarked that regardless if the accusation was true, which I did not believe in the first place, it was being spread out of malicious envy of this prominent couple. I felt it was a great teaching opportunity to speak life back to the tale-bearer.

There was no truth in the tale, but because of the gossip being spread about them, there was great devastation to the couple, both personally between the two of them, as well as their children, and close family and friends. Damage done from careless words.

James knew how very destructive the tongue was in the early church. There was division, strife, jealousy, and every kind of evil. His counsel to the church was to be aware of the danger of the tongue. In these verses, he tells us the weight of responsibility we carry in the use of our words. Do our words bring life and healing, or are they a poisonous venom with death in its wake?

When my girls were younger and they would tattle on each other or their friends, I would ask them: is it kind, necessary, or true? Of course, if there was something serious, I wanted to know about it. However, there is a difference between sharing something to prevent a potential problem or disaster over sharing something to purposefully get someone in trouble or knowingly sow seeds of discord.

James talks about the heart condition throughout the entire book. Going back to James 1:26, he states, "If anyone thinks he is religious without controlling his tongue, then his religion is useless, and he deceives himself." Unfortunately, we have seen firsthand what happens when someone in the church says something that does more damage than good in responding to their "online presence" on Facebook or Instagram. No one has ever been won to Christ by arguing on social media (or even in person!). In fact, it often has the opposite effect.

A person who practices true religion, the kind James is talking about in these verses, is able to control the whole body. That person is a mature Christian and allows himself to be guided by the Holy Spirit. It is the wisdom of the Spirit that guides this mature individual through his works, good behavior, gentleness, peace-loving, compliant, and merciful conduct. Is this you? Rather than carelessly hurling your words, do you stop and ask God for wisdom on how to respond or if you even need to respond? Next time take a moment to pray in the situation and see how God leads you. Jesus is our perfect example of what to say, when to say it, and how to say it, or even if it needs to be spoken at all.

If you aren't sure if you are being a shining example of controlling your tongue, examine your posts on Facebook (have you ever won anyone to Christ by what you've posted?). Think about the last time you were behind someone on their phone at a green light, and, by the time you were able to go through, the light changed and you had to sit through another round of red lights (did you do some name-calling or fume in exasperation at the inconvenience?). What about when someone in your family ate a special treat you bought for yourself or that someone gave you? Did you passive aggressively show your displeasure?

Once the words have been spoken, you can't take them back. They will forever float about in the mind of the one who was on the other end of the conversation. I still remember hateful and hurtful things spoken to me and about me from my teen years. Words cut deep and leave scars. Just like a little spark can set a forest on fire, our words can destroy and devastate.

James doesn't keep us feeling badly about our lack of controlling the tongue. He gives us hope that through the Spirit, we can walk in maturity and self-control over this little member of our body. Reading to the end of the chapter gives us this encouragement we need. James 3:18 closes with, "And the fruit of righteousness is sown in peace by those who cultivate peace."

Since we are all designed and created in the likeness of God, I encourage you today to ask God to help you see others in His image. As you begin to see as God sees, pray that God will give you the wisdom you need to control your tongue. In controlling your tongue, examine your heart. It is out of the heart-itude that your words overflow. May God bless you with a heart like His.

Reflection

Have your words been true, kind and necessary?

In what ways have you been setting your world on fire with your words?

Are you following the wisdom of godly self-control in the use of your words?

Perhaps you are guilty of using your words negatively in your "online presence" or using your words to promote yourself at home, work, or church. Ask God to show you where your words are creating fires that are destroying entire forests.

Meditate on Psalm 19:14 "May the words of my mouth and the meditation of my heart be acceptable to You, Lord, my rock and my Redeemer."

HEROES DON'T NEED PAPARAZZI

Benaiah son of Jehoiada was the son of a brave man from Kabzeel, a man of many exploits. Benaiah killed two sons of Ariel of Moab, and he went down into a pit on a snowy day and killed a lion. He also killed an Egyptian, a huge man. Even though the Egyptian had a spear in his hand, Benaiah went down to him with a club, snatched the spear out of the Egyptian's hand, and then killed him with his own spear. These were the exploits of Benaiah son of Jehoiada, who had a reputation among the three warriors. He was the most honored of the Thirty, but he did not become one of the Three. David put him in charge of his bodyguard.

2 Samuel 23:20-23

There's a hero in my family. His days of being a hero started back when we were kids, and he fought to protect me from bullies and unsavory characters at school and at work. It's my brother. He is younger than me, but often in these situations, he became a fierce older brother, protecting those who were weaker and standing up to the "giants" in our lives. One time, he protected our younger brother from a neighborhood bully, and hurt himself in the process, but he didn't stop protecting us until the bully had finally retreated from the playground.

As he grew into adulthood, he became a devoted husband and father to a daughter and two sons. At one point in his life, my brother felt called into the ministry and began pursuing his seminary education, but then God called him into another area, that of a soldier. He's been in many battles, endured heartache and challenges that face a military family, and yet, through all of it, his loyalty to his position and his country drive him as a soldier and a commander.

My brother still is a hero both on and off the battlefield. His men adore him, and his family loves him. He commands the respect of hundreds of soldiers and has more schooling under his belt than I can even comprehend. I've noticed something about heroes, though. With each homecoming, my brother has shied away from the paparazzi of being in the limelight, quietly standing with his men, not wanting a fuss to be made over him. True heroes do what they are called to do, when they are called to do it, and give it their all. In fact, when others comment about his commendations, awards, ribbons, and pins, he ducks his head, grins a little, and just shakes his head. "It's all in the line of duty."

We see a great hero of faith that behaves much the same way in 2 Samuel. There are only a few verses that mention him, but what is written about him is all we need to know to understand that he is considered a hero, doing his job well, and is loyal to the end.

Benaiah was born into the priestly lineage. According to 1 Chronicles 27:5, Benaiah's father, Jehoiada was a priest. However, Benaiah was called out of the priest-hood to become a soldier. His exploits were remarkable, and he performed valiantly on the battlefield in hand to hand combat, fighting with only a club in one instance, disarming his opponent and killing him with the ene-my's own weapon.

Benaiah is probably best known for doing a hard thing in a hard place in harsh conditions: killing a lion in a pit while it was snowing. His ability to maneuver in the pit was severely hampered, but he successfully killed the lion and claimed fame to this in a verse in the Bible.

Later, Benaiah's loyalty to King David was well known and later supported King David's son, Solomon, when he came to the throne years later. Although Bena-iah was not counted as one of the three warriors of David, he was honored among the Thirty Mighty Men of Valor. As he continued to serve his king faithfully, he later was promoted by Solomon to be the head of his army, taking Joab's place after Joab was executed (I Kings 2:34-35).

We see in these verses that this priestly soldier's fame doesn't end with his many exploits in battle on and off the field, but that he is also remembered as the father to Jehoiada who later became King Solo-mon's counselor (1 Chronicles 27:34). There isn't much said about his role as a father; however, to have a son rise high in the ranks as the king's counselor is pretty impressive. He must have done something right.

As we serve our King and the Kingdom of God here on Earth, we need to be careful to follow the humility of true heroes that have gone before us. We must follow the humility of Christ who did not seek to draw attention to Himself, but humbled Himself in order to exalt His Father, God. He didn't go looking for the paparazzi to record each time He served or healed.

True heroes don't consider themselves, rather they consider the ones they serve. They do it humbly and willingly. Their sacrifice is honorable.

True heroes don't need paparazzi.

Reflection

Do you have a hero in your family? Military, emergency services, law enforcement, or other civil servants? Take a moment and pray for them, for their protection, and for their families.

How could you better serve those who serve you?

Do you serve without thought of recognition or accolades? If this is what drives you to serve, examine your need for this.

If no one but God knows what you do, is this sufficient?

Stop seeking the spotlight and focus on your calling. God will reward you greatly. Perhaps you will get your chance to shine here on Earth but think of the audience you will have in Heaven as you are rewarded for your faithful and virtuous life...an audience with Jesus Christ, Himself!

FREEDOM TO LIVE FREE

Christ has liberated us to be free. Stand firm then and don't submit again to a yoke of slavery...For you were called to be free, brothers, only don't use this freedom as an opportunity for the flesh, but serve one another through love. For the entire law is fulfilled in one statement: Love your neighbor as yourself.

Galatians 5:1, 13-14

Ask people what "freedom" means to them. You will get varied answers, but the underlying theme would be "the right to speak, act, or think without restraint." Man, in his sinful nature, desires the ability to do what they want, when they want, and without thought of how their actions affect others. Just watch a two- or a three- year old when they have a playdate. You can see this principle unfold as the toys are brought out or snack time is announced. It usually doesn't matter what the toy or the snack is. If you have it, I want it, at any cost because it will make me happy.

I observed this for many years as I taught three-year-old preschoolers. In fact, I taught in two different states and the behaviors are remarkably the same. No one needs to teach a three-year-old about their rights. It's natural and instinctive. Move forward in time to when that three-year-old becomes a teenager. Even when raised in a godly home, teenagers can often

flare into the three-year-old they once were, demanding their freedom and rights as whatever seems good
to them at that moment.

As Christian parents or teachers, we desire to mold
these children into mature adults. But what happens
when this doesn't happen? What kind of adults do these
entitled children grow into? How do they view their freedom of choice? Are they really, truly free? What about
you, dear friend? What is your idea of freedom?

Paul was writing to the Galatians about a problem
that was causing issues in the early church. They were
focusing on the issue of being circumcised as an obli-
gation to keep the whole law in addition to the Law of
Liberty that Christ offered through His sacrifice on the
cross and resurrection. However, Paul was writing to
them in order to help them understand that as a Christ
follower, they were offered grace and mercy where
the law only offered bondage to rules and regulations.
Paul's word picture here is one of a free slave putting
himself back under bondage again. It evokes a ludi-
crous decision that would not have happened. Once
freed, a slave would value their freedom and treat it
with great respect.

As sinners, we fall into the category of slavery to sin.
We yield to the lusts of the flesh and eyes, and pride of
life (I John 2:16). It's nearly impossible to escape a life
of slavery to these innate characteristics due to our sin
nature. However, God knew this. In fact, He planned to
rescue us from this slavery through the sacrifice of His

own Son, Jesus Christ. Jesus came to set us free from this bondage of sin and offer us freedom in Him.

Under the yoke of bondage to sin, our slavery is a hard life with burdens that are much too heavy. We can easily picture in our minds heavy laden beasts of burden submitting to their master's whip and harsh words. That is how sin has control over us. It's harsh, unyielding, and eventually leads to death. I have met people who struggle with the sins of lust, gluttony, pride, and their daily battle to these sinful chains in their lives wearies them. They deeply desire for these chains of sin to be broken and to live free from the bondage they find themselves in.

Freedom in Christ allows us to put on the yoke of Christ and walk in this freedom (Matthew 11:28-30). Picture Christ walking side by side with us, carrying the heaviest part of the yoke on His shoulders as we get the easy and light section. Christ's yoke allows us the freedom to fulfill His will, completely the opposite of the law's will of enslaving us.

When our daughter Kylie was very young, she was trying to carry a heavy suitcase. Dave asked her if he could help carry the suitcase, and she responded, "We do it together, Daddy." Dave, of course, took on the entire weight himself, but let Kylie keep holding the handle, letting her think she was carrying the majority of the weight. This is how we can view our freedom from the bondage of sin in our lives. Jesus is carrying all the weight—of every sin of every person that has ever been born or ever will be born. Allowing us the freedom to walk in His grace, a gift that we don't deserve, and mercy, not giving us what we truly deserve. We can then live in the freedom of the liberty He has given His true and faithful followers. We don't have to live in bondage to our sin. We've been made free in Christ.

It is also in this perfect law of liberty and freedom that we can allow the Spirit to enable us to fulfill the law of love. As free men and women in Christ, we now live in the freedom of fulfilling the calling Christ has in our lives: to live as Christ and to love as Christ. In liberty and love, we can serve Christ and others more fully. What an exciting prospect as we seek to be more Christlike in our lives. In doing this, we continue to build the church, the body of Christ!

Reflection

Are you living under the yoke of bondage to sin and self or the yoke of Christ?

Look up the following words and write the definitions:
Liberty

Yoke

Bondage

License

As you read the definitions, how does this change your perspective of Christ's yoke, "easy and light," versus the yoke of the "bondage of sin"? Have you been slow to embrace Christ's yoke? Why?

How are you going to live differently living under the yoke of Christ, knowing that it brings freedom and liberty?

A RADIANT RELATIONSHIP

As Moses descended from Mount Sinai with the two tablets of the testimony in his hands as he descended the mountain he did not realize that the skin of his face shone as a result of his speaking with the LORD... When Moses had finished speaking with them, he put a veil over his face. But whenever Moses went before the LORD to speak with Him, he would remove the veil until he came out. After he came out, he would tell the Israelites what he had been commanded, and the Israelites would see that Moses' face was radiant. Then Moses would put the veil over his face again until he went to speak with the LORD.

Exodus 34:29, 33-35

At dinner a couple of nights ago, my friends and I sat around a table sharing thoughts on a variety of topics. It was a wonderful time of conversation and comradery. We all had recently met a lovely young lady that had begun dating a son of one of the couples in our group. One of the men commented, "When I saw the expression on his face as he looked at her, I would say he was smitten." We all agreed that this young man was well on his way to being in love and it was written all over his face.

It's amazing what can be read from our faces. I went to the chiropractor the other day and the first thing Dr.

Abbi asked was, "Do you have a migraine right now?" I asked how she knew this since I tried to hide behind makeup and a humorous repartee. She said, "It's all over your face."

When my piano students come to my house, I can tell almost instantly if they've had a rough day or a good day. Looking at pictures of Kylie and Grant's wedding, you can see the radiance of their expression, especially when Grant saw Kylie for the first time in her wedding dress as she walked down the aisle towards him. I remember the look of complete love and adoration when Dave gazed at both of our daughters after they were born.

When Moses came down off of the mountaintop with the Lord (Yahweh), he was radiant from time spent with God the Father. His face was so radiant, that the Israelites and Aaron were afraid. Can you picture it in your spiritual imagination? Moses shining so brightly, radiating the essence of God's presence with him, that in order for others to look at him and be around him, he needed to wear a veil?

There are a couple schools of thoughts on the veil Moses wore. Perhaps Moses wore a veil so that the Children of Israel wouldn't see the glory fading from his visage when Moses wasn't with God. Isn't that true of us? When we haven't spent time with God, it shows. Our demeanor, language and actions show who and what we spend the majority of our time with. Moses spent time with God, but then when he wasn't with God, the radiance diminished (Exodus 34:33-35).

Or perhaps, the radiance of Moses allowed his face to glow in the glory of God's presence. We know that God allowed Moses to see His glory, but man cannot look on the face of God and live, so God covered Moses' eyes with His Hands and passed by Him, giving Moses only a glimpse of the backside of God (Exodus 33:18-23). Spending time with God would certainly have caused one's face to radiate!

I often wonder if God's glory is radiating off of my face. Can others tell that I've spent time with God, in His Word, in prayer? Does my face reflect the love and joy of my Savior? Does my visage give off the idea that I'm approachable and friendly? When I'm worshipping at church with other believers, can others tell if I'm truly believing what I'm singing, or am I just going through the motions?

Thinking back to when you met your spouse, how did your face react when you saw him or her? Does it reflect that early love now after years have passed? Think about when you first accepted Christ into your heart and life. Remember the joy and elation you felt knowing that your eternity is secure in Him? As you battle the life before you, how does it show on your face? Does it reflect a joy-filled follower of Christ?

Whatever the reason Moses wore a veil, we understand the importance that he did. He had been with God, Yahweh, and God's glorious presence was reflected into and onto Moses. Moses carried about that reflection of a personal intimate relationship with his Redeemer. How do I know this? Because God said so in Exodus 33:17, "The

LORD answered Moses, I will do this very thing you have asked, for you have found favor in My sight, and I know you by name."

Reflection

Does God know you by name? Do you belong to Him?

Does your face (your life, actions and words) reflect that you've spent time with Jehovah God? What is it reflecting?

FELLOWSHIP WITH MY FATHER

What was from the beginning, what we have heard, what we have seen with our eyes, what we have observed and have touched with our hands, concerning the Word of life-that life was revealed, and we have seen it and we testify and declare to you the eternal life that was with the Father and was revealed to us-what we have seen and heard we also declare to you, so that you may have fellowship along with us; and indeed our fellowship is with the Father and with His Son Jesus Christ. We are writing these things so that our joy may be complete.

1 John 1:1-4

Growing up, I spent a lot of time with my dad. Early on, though, he worked the third shift and attended college full time, but as I got into my pre-teen and teen years, Dad was more available. I look back on those times and cherish the memories we made. Often my brothers would be with us as we would cut and stack wood, go fishing, or take camping trips. I remember fondly the time we spent together. Not what we did or where we did it, but the joy I had in just *being* with my dad.

One of my favorite memories with my dad was during my tumultuous high school years. During this time of growing pains, I also struggled the most with my mom. We both were so similar that we would clash on occasion leaving us both battered and bruised in our hearts. Dad would step in and take me for a drive that almost always ended in an ice cream treat.

We would talk over whatever happened that day or why Mom and I argued. He would allow me the freedom to share my feelings, and then he would gently correct and offer wisdom from the Bible. Dad knew so many verses by memory and could apply a verse to each situation.

Later on, as I grew into adulthood and became a parent myself, I would find myself calling him for advice and counsel in different circumstances. Dad was a vice-president of a large company during the early life of our oldest daughter. I remember he would often answer the phone during his busy day with this statement, "Let me close my office door so I can focus on you."

Although time has passed and our roles have reversed a little since the death of my mom, we continue this practice. Whether I am taking my dad to doctor appointments or going shopping, we continue to share this ritual of getting an ice cream treat or cup of coffee and spending time just talking. It's a comforting tradition that brings my heart joy.

Not everyone is so fortunate to have an earthly father who lovingly raised them or who is still here on Earth to spend time with. However, as followers of Christ, we have a Heavenly Father, who loves us and wants to spend time with us, to fellowship with us. A description I heard of "fellowship" growing up was "two fellows in the same ship." I can imagine myself in a boat lazily drifting on the water with my Heavenly Father sitting there, listening to me pour out my heart to Him, while He gently offers correction and encouragement.

Fellowship is an important vocabulary word for Christians. Simply put, it means "to have things in common." When God sent His Son Jesus to live among men, Christ took on the human form of man so that He could live in fellowship with us. When He became our sin for us, He took all our sins, past, present and future, on Himself so that He could bridge the gap between sinful man and a Holy God. We then became "partakers of the divine nature" so we could have fellowship with God directly (2 Peter 1:4).

In 1 John 1, the author John is sharing the secret of fellowship with God and even with other believers. In verse 4, he says that he is writing "so that our joy may be complete" in pursuing a relationship with God and others. Preceding this verse, however, John is revealing to us that the life we are living is "real." It is hard, complicated, full of sorrow and challenges (v. 5-10), but that in all of this realness, our hope isn't found in the temporal things of Earth, but in the very real person of Jesus Christ. In the very real person of Jesus Christ, we can have a personal encounter with Him. We can fellowship with Him. And one day, we will be with Him.

In our humanness, we need God's presence in our lives. Through the gift of His Son, we can have a true relationship with Him and experience His Divine Presence. We may not have a great earthly example of a father, or our father may no longer be living, but we have the best and most joyful of all experiences with God as our Father. Continuing in 1 John 1, we see how we can continue to develop our relationship with God as we "walk in the light" (v. 7).

I love seeing my relationship with God lived out in the gift of nature. When the sun is shining on my face, I can sense the presence of God. In the beauty of all that is around me, I can see the glory God created to bring my heart joy in being in His presence. In the scents of baking and cooking, I imagine the presence of God and I'm a "sweet smelling sacrifice" made Holy to the Lord. God's presence is all around me in the "touchy feely" aspects of my world, but He is also present in my heart and soul as I experience depths of sorrow, joy, tears, and laughter.

It is in my relationship with God as my Father that I can experience a true, deep personal fellowship that culminates in great joy, the "real" relationship the Apostle John is writing about in these verses. Then, through my fellowship with God, I can have "real" relationships with my brothers and sisters in Christ, experiencing joy *with them*, through joy *in Him*.

In this we are complete.

Reflection

Describe your relationship with your earthly father. How is it the same or different from your relationship with your Heavenly Father?

Are you finding joy in your relationship with your Heavenly Father? Why or why not?

What are some ways you can experience the presence of God in your life today? Share some verses that you can meditate on to remind you of His presence.

COME WHAT MAY

Though the fig tree does not bud and there is no fruit on the vines, though the olive crop fails and the fields produce no food, though there are no sheep in the pen and no cattle in the stalls, yet I will triumph in Yahweh; I will rejoice in the God of my salvation! Yahweh my Lord is my strength; He makes my feet like those of a deer and enables me to walk on mountain heights!

Habakkuk 3:17-19

It was the year that the flood came. After several years of back to back difficulties, this storm culminated in a devastation that brought destruction and near financial ruin to our family. It was a "five year" program that God was using to bring us to our knees in surrender to Him, and it all came to a crashing conclusion that June 30th evening.

What started as a typical summer rain here in Iowa, gradually grew into "an inland tropical storm" with records of five inches of rain in an hour, flooding the streets, drains, and homes of hundreds of people, including us. We were helpless in the stemming of the floods that rushed down the apartment stairs (we lived in a lower level), the bubbling up of water as it came out of the bathtub drains and toilets, and through the windows as rain was pushed through any crevice that allowed it through.

The night carried on in thunderous crashes and brilliant lightning, only to taper off and give way to a glorious morning of blue skies and brilliant sunshine. A complete antithesis to what had come previously. It seemed unreal, except for the fact that we woke up in different beds with only the clothes on our backs as a harsh reminder of what had transpired only hours before. I stood in amazement at the complete transformation of weather, marveling in the awesome power God exhibited in the storm the night before and the peace that embraced the quiet morning dawn.

We lost just about everything we owned; our beds, our furniture, our clothes and shoes, the food in the refrigerator (we lost power during the storm), but we had each other, and we had our health. In this, we had all we needed to continue with "come what may." Although the storm had raged around us, we were able to rejoice in Him.

God allowed us to find humor as we cleaned out the flooded apartment. He brought friends to our rescue to help load what possessions were salvageable. God brought meals through gift cards, homemade dinners, and carry-out lunches. God knew that our fragile hurting hearts needed the reassurance that, even while our world had crumbled around us, He was still present, working in our hearts and lives, strengthening us, and encouraging us through the people who ministered to us that week and in the weeks to come.

Habakkuk understood, too, what it meant to have his world crashing about him. He lived in a time when Babylon had nearly destroyed all of Judah and there wasn't much left at all to rejoice in during the aftermath of a crashed economy, devastated farms, vineyards and orchards, as well as the destruction of personal property, treasures, and even loss of life (2:17).

Yet, in all this, Habakkuk was able to declare victory in the Lord, rejoicing in the God of his salvation. He boasted that the "Lord is my strength; He makes my feet like those of a deer and enables me to walk on mountain heights." Not only was he rejoicing, he was skipping and prancing in delight because God was his salvation and strength at a time when Habakkuk needed God to carry him through the desperate trials of affliction.

How often we tend to feel and react the opposite way when difficulties arise. We may grumble and complain (I know I have!), asking God, "Why us?" A godly mentor once asked me, "*Why not* us?" That question caused some deep introspective considering. Looking at others and seeing their prosperity and deliverance, we may grow jealous of their situation, wondering why God is pouring out challenges to us and not them.

Regardless of our situation (or our neighbor's), God is still on the throne. He is our Yahweh, Jehovah, and Salvation as Habakkuk reminds us in these verses. God continues to be victorious in all He accomplishes here on Earth, and when He chooses to use us as a vessel of opportunity to bring Him glory, we should mirror the image that Habakkuk gives us, rejoicing, prancing, skipping, and jumping in our walk through the valley as well as on the mountaintop!

Reflection

Can you say, "Come what may," and rejoice as Habakkuk shares with us in these verses?

What keeps you from fully giving your life, trials, and blessings, over to God and allowing Him to work in your life?

Reflect on a time when God brought you through a difficulty with abundant blessings and record it here. Thank God for His provision in this time of need and ask Him for strength for what you are facing today.

Ask God to give you feet like deer so that you can rejoice on the mountaintop in rejoicing!

WHEN THINGS GO WRONG

God is our refuge and strength, a helper who is always found in times of trouble. Therefore, we will not be afraid, though the earth trembles and the mountains topple into the depths of the seas, though its waters roar and foam and the mountains quake with its turmoil. *Selah*

Psalm 46:1-3

Reading back through my journals from years past, I've picked up on a theme running through them. Lots of things have gone wrong, or not gone our way, in our lives. We've experienced deep hurt, rejection, and pain. Some of the things that have gone wrong that make it into our top ten list are:
- Nine years making a career decision
- College debt
- Infertility, miscarriages, and death of a stillborn
- Unresolved heath issues
- Thirteen moves in nine years
- Marriage difficulties
- Financial challenges
- Church problems
- Weather-related devastation
- Relationship problems among close friends

Not only have things gone wrong, but I admit to many personal failings. I wonder if you've got some "failures" that I've listed:

- Lack of forgiveness
- Jealousy of others
- Critical speech or unwise words
- Unappreciative of blessings
- Non-demonstrative towards my husband (or God)
- Lack of submission to God (or my husband)
- Anger

That's quite the list. For me, when I read these confessions, I fall back into a pattern of guilt and remorse over past decisions, transgressions, and sins. It seems like it's insurmountable to overcome these troubles that seem to shake our world.

However, when things go wrong in relationships, jobs, church responsibilities, and the world, I can find shelter in God's presence. Sometimes, I just don't know who to turn to here on Earth that can make things right or even understand my emotional upheavals, but I know that I can take refuge in God's strength during these uncertainties. He not only knows what I'm experiencing, He knows what I'm thinking and feeling.

In this world, we will find ourselves in "times of trouble," backed into the proverbial corner, and, sometimes, we just can't find a way out. Despite all the circumstances that surround us, the earth trembling, the mountains toppling, the water roaring and foaming, and the mountains quaking, we can find refuge in

God as our refuge, shelter, and rock. As the psalmist continues in verses 7 and 11, "He is our stronghold, a high tower, and our fortress. He is with us."

Life's circumstances are always changing, sometimes slowly and other times so quickly we don't see it coming. Looking back since the COVID Pandemic of March 2020 as it morphed into civil outrage and riots in May, I'm stunned at all that has transpired in only a few short months. Then, in August, the Midwest experienced a devastating Derecho that wiped out crops, buildings, homes, and businesses, leaving many without power, water, or a place to live. But in all these things, God never changes, His covenant of peace and love will not be removed or shaken due to our circumstances (Isaiah 54:10). He wasn't surprised by any of it.

There are times that I do feel like God's "just not there": when I pray and I don't receive an answer, when I cry out in anguish and receive no peace, and when trials come, and they just don't seem to end. In these times of crises, I tend to rely on my own self-sufficiency, the counsel of others, or retreat into a good book or binge watch my favorite show. Much like the author of this psalm, the historical background is during a time when King Hezekiah was on the throne at a time when the Assyrians were planning an attack on the southern kingdom, Judah.

Assyrians were well known for their brutality and terror, so King Hezekiah's fear was understandable. God wasn't taken by surprise at what was going to happen (2 Kings 18-19). He is an omniscient, all knowing Heavenly Father. Even when things go wrong, as they often will, they never catch God unaware. That is why we can rest in the words of the psalmist, "God is my refuge and strength, a helper who is always found in times of trouble."

Do not be afraid He whispered to me
As I sat upon bended knee
Crying out my fear and dread
He said Dear Child, look to Me instead
The world may change and the mountains may fall
But I AM the One in control of it all
The waters may rise and wash over the land
But on My promises you can stand
I am Your Helper always right by your side
Whether duties or dangers, I will always abide
As your Refuge, your Rock, your Shelter to cling
A Mighty Fortress is my God, I will shout and sing

TAMPER THE TEMPER

A gentle answer turns away anger, but a harsh word stirs up wrath. The tongue of the wise makes knowledge attractive, but the mouth of fools blurts out foolishness.

Proverbs 15:1-2

He said. She said. He was wounded. She was hurt. Words were hurled and uttered without thought, arrows that pierced the heart, drawing blood. Wounds become infected and cause internal damage. You don't see the scars, they are hidden from view, but evident to anyone who hears the words. The infection never cared for poisons the whole body and poisons the heart.

In the book of James, the author writes about how the tongue is a restless evil to those who don't learn how to control its deadly poison (James 3:8). If you ever wonder if your heart is a bitter or sweet spring of water, listen to yourself in an argument. Are you spewing out words that are intended to hurt and maim, or are your words a healing medicine?

The writer of Proverbs realized how important it is to control one's tongue, especially when a person is angry. His encouragement to offer soft words during a time of great emotional distress counsels us to have a gentle spirit and practice self-control (Galatians 5:22-23). It's not our goal in life to prove ourselves right, but to bring honor and glory to God through the power of our words. In fact, the writer is sharing his learned wisdom in having the correct attitude when dealing with someone who is angry. A soft answer is a step to making peace and settling a matter calmly.

Wisdom is necessary in our lives as we live with and love those around us. Wisdom in our speech goes far deeper than just surface level. Our words are an indication of what is in our hearts (James 3:14). Those words revealed are a reflection of our wisdom or our foolishness, but most of all where our wisdom comes from. Is it earthly or from above (James 3:17)? Our words have the power of life and death in them. Since we are made in the likeness of God, who communicates to us through His Word and the power of the Holy Spirit, how much more should we pattern our speech after the One who created us?

When I was growing up, my Dad used to say to us, "Better to remain silent and be thought a fool than to speak and remove all doubt" (Abraham Lincoln).[4] The picture here of a fool is one who acts like a windbag, full of hot air but lacking in sense and substance, blurting out whatever he wishes, without thought of anyone else, who he is hurting and his evident lack of self-control.

The wise man can be angry and not sin. The wise man knows when to speak and when to hold his tongue. Just because he doesn't speak in an argument doesn't mean he's giving in or compromising the truth. As he has learned through God's Word, a soft answer can defuse a situation to a degree for when communication can actually take place.

In the book of Proverbs, we learn that our words have value and can bring healing, nourishment, and beauty as we use them to bring peace, restoration, and refreshment to those we come into contact with, often being an example of love to the lives of unbelievers. As we live like Christ, our words should reflect Christ's humility.

Growing older, I see wisdom in learning to control one's words and tampering down the temptation to temper. I've seen out of control tempers do so much damage that family members haven't spoken to each other in over fifty years. It breaks my heart when I hear older people say, "Now that I'm this old, I feel like I've earned the right to say exactly what I feel, and I don't care what others think." This isn't what God teaches us in His Word. However, I've also seen how the gentle spirit that responds quietly and with wisdom is able to repair broken relationships and restore wayward brothers and sisters to the Lord.

Let our words be attractive, pleasing to God as well as to others. Let our words reflect godly wisdom, putting into practice the Fruit of the Spirit. Let our words be a healing balm to the wounded. Let our hearts be in a position of prayerful consideration as we communicate with one another, so that in all of this, the Lord would be glorified by the words we speak.

BITTER BETRAYAL

Jesus replied, "He's the one I give the piece of bread to after I have dipped it." When He had dipped the bread, He gave it to Judas, Simon Iscariot's son. After Judas ate the piece of bread, Satan entered him. Therefore, Jesus told him, "What you're doing, do quickly."

John 13:26-27

Early in our marriage, Dave and I experienced firsthand the sting of bitter betrayal in our lives. We moved around quite a bit, and each new place held its own set of challenges. One of the most difficult times we faced was a problem within our church's leadership. As a young couple, we were hesitant to ruffle feathers or cause a disruption, but as time went on, the problems grew to a crescendo, and the Holy Spirit would not let us stay quiet any longer.

After a series of meetings, a respected member of the congregation and an elder in the church called a meeting between the pastor and us, all the while assuring us of his complete support, agreeing that we did indeed have cause to be concerned over the doctrinal issues that were being preached from the pulpit. The day arrived, and the elder prayed over us before the meeting; then the meeting ensued. Within minutes, there had been a complete shift in the dynamic, and we were proverbially thrown to the wolves. Cue the gnashing teeth and snarling.

Walking away from that meeting, our spirits were sorrowful and abused Heavy hearted, we reached out to God, asking for discernment and clarification from the meeting. Praying God would reveal to us any sinful way we might have walked during this time, we were left firmly convinced that we had represented God well, but we were battered and bruised. The wounds stung, cutting us deeply.

Since our first experience dealing with bitter betrayal, I've heard many stories of bitter betrayal in marital infidelity, sibling rivalry, family feuds, parents disowning or abandoning their own children, friendships dissolved, and dishonest business dealings. One sibling rivalry story that left me stunned was one about two brothers who didn't speak for over fifty years because of something "he said." I have personally watched family members being disowned by their own parents. It is a poisonous gall to drink, this bitter betrayal of those we trust to have our good in mind only to discover that they do not.

Bitter betrayal can leave wounds that go deep, and, if left undealt with, can become infected and fester, poisoning the body, spilling out onto others around us. It is enough to make your heart hurt in the worst kind of way. Life as you once knew it to be, rocked to the core, making you question things you've known to be true. How can this be? How can two people, who were at one time devoted to each other, be torn apart? How can friends be so divided? How can parents turn their backs on their children?

Reading through the Bible, we read examples of betrayal, lies, and deceit. Some died because of it. Some lost their fortunes. But this one truth stands above the rest: each one lost—they all lost someone they once dearly loved. Cain lost Abel (Genesis 4). Jacob lost Esau (Genesis 25). Joseph lost his brothers (Genesis 37). Absalom lost King David. King David lost Ahithophel (2 Samuel 15-17). Jesus lost Judas (John 13).

In Psalm 41:9, the psalmist expresses his deep hurt and devastation caused by ultimate betrayal in a close, trusted friend: "Even my friend in whom I trusted, one who ate my bread, has raised his heel against me." Job even experienced the ultimate hurt of betrayal as "all of my best friends despise me, and those I love have turned against me" (Job 19:19).

It's hard to even contemplate such treachery, but even Jesus experienced betrayal by a close friend, one with whom He spent three years of His life mentoring, teaching, sharing, eating, and doing ministry together. Judas had been hand chosen by Jesus as one of the twelve disciples. Judas was a respected individual among the twelve, carrying around the "checkbook" and managing the finances.

Something stands out clearly to me as I read these verses. Even in the midst of Judas's impending treachery, Jesus continued to protect him. He never revealed to the other disciples the role Judas would play in

Jesus's crucifixion. Even when Jesus told Judas, "To go do it quickly," the others thought it had something to do with Judas providing for the poor (John 13:27-20).

Why would Jesus go out of His way to protect the very person who would hand Him over to the authorities? I believe there are two reasons for Jesus's continued protection of Judas.

First, Jesus had come to fulfill the Word of God and magnify the glory of God (John 13:18-35). Jesus knew that His death was a vital part of the plan for the redemption of the world. It was through this final perfect sacrifice that mankind could be reconciled to the Holy God. Jesus knew He had to die.

Secondly, Jesus loved His disciples. His love and concern for them kept Him from revealing the treachery of Judas. It's possible that through Judas, their faith would be weakened or that they might do something impetuous and impede the plan of God. Peter, the outspoken member of the group, even cut off the ear of the servant when Jesus was being arrested (John 18:10). Just think of the possibilities that might have occurred had the disciples known of Judas's betrayal to come. It could have had devastating repercussions.

Despite the bitter betrayal, Jesus was still in control. He was still determined to "do the will of His Father." He stands as the perfect example to us of the recipient of betrayal. Jesus continued to be the Light of the World and the Lamb as He walked through the days leading to His death.

Just before this time at the dinner table, Jesus had washed the disciples' feet. The twelve disciples, Judas included. But lest you think that Jesus was spiritualizing the situation, pretending to be above the hurt and disappointment that comes with betrayal, look at verse 21 where it said that Jesus was "troubled in His spirit." Jesus knew He was being completely rejected by one whom He loved. It bothered Him deeply.

Jesus understands our pain of betrayal. He's been through it Himself. Yet He continued to pour out His love and glorify His Father. Jesus didn't begin to slander the one who walked away. He turned His love to those who remained. A very potent reminder to us to continue in love: love for Him and love for others, so that despite cruel betrayal, the evidence will speak loudly on our behalf of our love for one another (1 John 3:16).

Reflection

Have you been betrayed by someone you loved? How did you respond?

Did your response create greater issues or open the doors for future reconciliation?

I encourage you to take your hurt, anger, and sadness to the Lord. Ask Him to help you forgive the one who betrayed you. Watch how God will bring healing to your heart.

IVORY SOAP AND A TACK ROOM

So he came closer and kissed him. When Isaac smelled his clothes, he blessed him and said: Ah, the smell of my son is like the smell of a field that the Lord has blessed.

Genesis 27:27

The smell hit me from a forty year memory—the aroma of horses, leather, hay, and oil. My grandpa's tack room still looked and smelled the same even though his farm had been sold nearly twenty years before. The new owners knew our family and allowed us a final walkthrough of the barn and house before the house was torn down. My dad had lived there nearly his entire life, and I spent much of my childhood summers visiting my grandma after my grandpa passed away from cancer.

The beautifully rustic old red barn had never been updated, so the rusty hinge of the door handle still groaned as I opened the door. When the smell came rushing out to meet me, I instantly began to cry. The memories were so powerful it was if I could smell my grandpa after a long day of working with the horses. I saw his weather-beaten face, lined and worn, but it was his eyes that always captured my attention. Behind his rough cowboy exterior were gentle blue eyes.

Making my way up the slight hill to the house where my grandma lived for thirteen years after Grandpa was gone, I saw the overrun flowerbeds, the cats that seemed to congregate by the back door just as they had done years before, and the same well-used screen door that never seemed to latch. Inside the front porch was the same nail with the key on it, just in case someone needed to get inside and grab a bite to eat. Opening the back door, memories flooded my mind and overpowered my heart. There were those tears again. And the smell! The Ivory Soap smell still lingered in the front hall.

The smell of the house, musty from years of being shut up, still smelled like my childhood. Grandma always washed with Ivory Soap. Her face and hands were fragrant with that scent. Even when she was nearing death, I could smell the Ivory Soap on her skin. I closed my eyes and saw Grandma standing at the old sink. Water from the well smelled like iron, and there were iron stains still in the sink. I couldn't go any further because the floor was rotten, but oh! Precious memories of two very special people in my life were brought back to life through the gift of scent.

I imagine as Isaac neared the end of his life and as his eyesight faded, smells became very important to him. He knew the smell of his eldest son. He knew the feel of his hairy arms. He knew this son would make him the tastiest stew. He just knew this was his son. As an old man, this brought comfort to him as he was ready to bestow the blessing on him. The eldest son got the blessing.

But then Isaac realized he had been tricked. This is perhaps the greatest tragedy of this entire family debacle. Isaac's senses had failed him, and, unwittingly, he bestowed the blessing to his youngest son, Jacob, the trickster. Jacob, with the help of his Mother, Rebekah, prepared the stew just as Esau would have done. Then Rebekah dressed Jacob in Esau's clothing, adding skins of young goats where Jacob's smooth skin might give him away since Esau was a hairy man. And the two of them set out to deceive Isaac and steal the birthright from Esau.

The deception was complete, and the blessing was given to the youngest son. In walks the eldest son, with a new stew prepared, ready to be a blessing to his father and receive a blessing, only to find out the right to rule the family had been given to the wrong son. Isaac, well over 100 years old, realized what has transpired. Esau begged for a blessing from his father. This tragic family drama had severe and devastating consequences. It tore the family apart in ways that took over twenty years to repair, but the damage was done. In the end, the blessing did not satisfy Jacob.

God tells us that "we are the fragrance of Christ among those who are being saved...an aroma of life leading to life" (2 Corinthians 2:15-16). Smell is important to God. In the Old Testament, we read many times of how different burnt offerings were considered "a sweet-smelling savor" to God. Our lives lived for Him to produce the scent of Christ, a fragrance that only

Jesus Christ could produce through His obedience and sacrifice on the cross.

Apostle Paul writes in Ephesians 5:2 that as we "walk in love, as the Messiah also loved us and gave Himself for us, a sacrificial and fragrant offering to God," the fragrance we "wear" is our imitation of Christ's love. And again, in Philippians 4:18, Paul is reminding the church at Philippi of the "fragrant offering, an acceptable sacrifice, pleasing to God" that had been sent from Epaphroditus as he lived out his love by providing abundantly for the Apostle Paul.

Smells can be wonderful tools of memory, reminders of those we loved best who have been taken from us, or they can be reminders of choices made in sin with tragic consequences. We as believers can bear two different results, two different scents to two different groups of people. To the unbelievers, we bear the scent of death, as they reject the gift of salvation, they perish. To the believers, we bear the scent of life as we share the gospel of Christ and they receive this fragrant offering.

> Sight, hearing, feeling, taste and smell,
> Are gifts we highly prize,
> But these may downward lead to hell,
> While faith to heav'n doth rise.
> ~John Newton[5]

ARE YOU AVAILABLE?

Jesus answered, "If you knew the gift of God, and who is saying to you, 'Give Me a drink,' you would ask Him, and He would give you living water." "Sir," said the woman, "You don't even have a bucket, and the well is deep. So where do You get this 'living water'? You aren't greater than our father Jacob, are You? He gave us the well and drank from it himself, as did his sons and livestock." Jesus said, "Everyone who drinks from this water will get thirsty again. But whoever drinks from the water that I will give him will never get thirsty again-ever! In fact, the water I will give him will become a well of water springing up within him for eternal life."

John 4:10-14

The phone rang, and I was truly just too busy to answer. I hesitated a few more moments to pick up, knowing it was going to be a lengthy phone call, and I was trying to get so many things accomplished. I almost missed an opportunity to be Jesus to someone that day.

I had been looking forward to a long massage since my accident, dealing with whiplash and low back pain. All I wanted to do was lay there in silence and allow her healing hands to massage the knots in my neck away. I almost missed an opportunity to share the gospel that day.

Getting groceries isn't my favorite thing to do, and I wanted to get in and out quickly to get to my next appointment. The older gentleman in front of me seemed so lonely and wanted someone to talk to about the weather and his grandchildren. I almost missed the opportunity to share the love of Jesus.

Hurrying to put up the chairs and tables after Bible study so I could get home and eat lunch, the new woman announced she would help me put things away, but she wanted to talk about where she just moved from and what drew her to our women's Bible study. I almost missed an opportunity to be the hands and feet of Jesus.

Jesus embraced His mission here on Earth by being available to those who needed Him. Sometimes it was healing, or the raising of their dead. Sometimes, it was providing lunch to thousands of people or using teaching moments with His disciples. But one thing is very evident by the accounts of the Lord throughout the Gospels: Jesus made Himself available. He didn't rush things, hurrying to get through the crowds or hide behind a rack of camel skins so that He didn't have to minister to someone in need because He "had other things to do."

That's why I absolutely love the story about the Woman at the Well. Jesus had just been traveling for many days, leaving Judea and coming back into Galilee. However, He opted for the most direct route, and that led Him straight through Samaria. (Gasp! A devout Jew would travel further and longer just to avoid this country!) Jesus was tired, weary and worn from His journey, and His disciples were hungry. In fact, I'd venture to say they were "hangry," hungry bordering on anger, as was evident by their insistence that Jesus eat something in verse 31, "In the meantime the disciples kept urging Him, 'Rabbi, eat something.'"

The Samaritan woman that Jesus met at the well was astounded that a Jewish man would even deign to speak to her, let alone ask her for a drink of water. The Samaritans were considered lowly, unclean, and unworthy of association by the Jews, even referred to as "dogs." So Jesus' conversation with her was startling to say the least. Not only did He speak to her and ask for a drink, He began to have a conversation with her.

Her response was immediate. She knew her historical tradition of Jacob's well, whether it is actual fact or not, and was ready to share her knowledge with this stranger. Jesus, not deterred or in a hurry, continued to talk to her, drawing her out in conversation. As the dialogue continues through the next few verses, Jesus asks the Samaritan woman questions, she answers with half-truths, and then He begins to reveal Himself to her. She is amazed and excited, declaring that He must be a prophet, even going so far to exclaim that she "knows that Messiah is coming (who is called Christ). When He comes, He will explain everything to us." That's when Jesus proclaims Himself to be the Messiah.

I can picture this entire scene in my imagination. Jesus, leaning against the well, the Samaritan woman with a pitcher on her head and a hand on her hip, carrying on this conversation as the disciples walk closer and closer, realizing that Jesus is talking to a woman—and not just any woman, a Samaritan woman. The looks on their faces might have been comical, except for the fact that Jesus came to "seek and save that which is lost," and she was indeed lost.

Just then, the woman forgets her original chore of getting water, puts down her pitcher and runs towards town to tell everyone she knows that the Messiah is at the well. The disciples begin to chastise Jesus for two reasons. One is that He needed food, and two was that He is talking to a woman! Not even in the Jewish society did a man even talk to his own wife because it diverted his attention away from the study of Scripture.

However, Jesus was on a mission. His mission was more important to Him than food or water. He was about His Father's work and the fields were ready for harvest (v. 25). Jesus was available to talk with one woman, and ultimately, many from that town believed in Him, and the harvest was ready! This woman excitedly left her water jar and ran into the town to share what "this man" had told her and followed her back to where Jesus was standing (John 4:28-30). Many Samaritans believed that day because of the woman's testimony, but more than that, they believed because they had heard and witnessed Jesus for themselves, understanding that He is the Savior of the world. The harvest was ready (John 4:39-42).

I wonder how many times I have missed opportunities to be about my Father's work because I was in a hurry, had "things to do" and was unavailable. How many times did I miss out on the work Jesus has called me to do through planting, sowing, and harvesting? I need to "open my eyes and look at the fields, for they are ready for harvest" (v. 35).

Lord, it is my prayer that you would allow me to live in a state of being available to do the work you have called me to do. Lead me to those who are standing at Your well, desiring a drink of Living Water. Allow me the honor of planting, sowing, or reaping today. Amen!

NO EARTHLY FATHER

For this Melchizedek-King of Salem, priest of the Most High God, who met Abraham and blessed him as he returned from dating the kings, and Abraham gave him a tenth of everything; first, his name means king of righteousness, then also, king of Salem, meaning king of peace; without father, mother or genealogy, having neither beginning of days nor end of life, but resembling the Son of God-remains a priest forever.

Hebrews 7:1-3

She never knew her dad. All her childhood she dreamed about an invisible person she didn't know. There was no name, no image, nothing. Julia had an earthly step-father who loved her and supplied for her needs, but the gnawing at her heart to know her biological father ate away at her. Finally, as an adult, she began the process of trying to locate her biological father and stepped into a journey of self-discovery of who she really was.

As a Christ follower, she rested in the assurance of her Heavenly Father. He walked with her daily, and as her desire for their biological father grew, so did her relationship with her Heavenly Father. The search began. It was fraught with disappointment and very few answers. Her mother had passed away when Julia was in her teens. She looked nothing like her mother, so the emptiness of that missing element haunted her each time she looked in the mirror.

Who am I? Why do I look like this? Why didn't my father want me? Why hasn't he tried to find me? Questions like these plagued her constantly. When she began to have children, they looked just like her, and the empty hole grew. Days and weeks turned into months and years. The search continued. The desire to know was an insatiable appetite. Until one day, a vital piece of the puzzle clicked into place, and one small answer led to a very large answer.

She found her father! After using several ancestry tools and DNA testing, she began to receive little pieces of her puzzle. After a year and a half searching for information, she received the vital puzzle piece. A phone call was placed, and a connection was made. Finally, Julia was able to have some of her questions answered. Fearing she had been rejected as a child, she discovered that her father didn't even know she existed. Since she didn't resemble her mom at all, her ethnicity and physical attributes made sense as she stared into the eyes of her father. She looked just like him and her new stepsiblings. The gaping pieces of the puzzle began to fill in and she had a full picture.

While she was searching for her earthly father, she had become more dependent on her Heavenly Father. Julia rested in the fact that even if she never discovered the truth about her earthly father, her Heavenly Father was always there for her, loving and providing for her. When she met her earthly father for the first time, it was if God was allowing her to experience Him in a much deeper way in love, acceptance and hope in a future life together.

Not everyone gets the answers they desire to know about their biological parents. Not every answer is a good answer. The potential of heartbreak is real and present even as searches are over. Some never get to know. The hole in their heart is gaping, unfilled, empty. Sadly, this unfulfilled desire reflects in an individual's life and it can be hard to push forward, to find one's purpose and calling, and to really live a full and vibrant life. But it doesn't have to be this way. We have a real life example that experienced not having parents and became a very successful person and important enough to have a record in our Bible.

In Genesis 14, we meet a man named Melchizedek. He is the King of Salem and a priest to the Patriarch, Abraham. Melchizedek is also without father, mother, or genealogy. There's not much known about him outside of a few verses that record his name, his profession, and his relationship with God. It's in his name we understand that Melchizedek means king of righteousness and peace. Despite his upbringing, Melchizedek chose to embrace the Most High God and serve Him in a lifelong commitment.

Melchizedek was an Old Testament representation of Jesus Christ who is our King-Priest. Through Him, we can enjoy righteousness and peace as we serve Him in our daily lives. Whether or not Melchizedek ever knew his parents, he had a Heavenly Father he chose to live for and reflect in his behavior and beliefs. Jesus Christ is our perfect representation of righteousness and peace, and we, too, can choose to emulate Him in our lives as well.

Not only did Melchizedek follow and obey God, he served those around him generously. Abraham had just come back from battle. We can spiritually imagine that Abraham and his men were exhausted, weary, and worn from their fighting. What did Melchizedek do? He offered them bread and wine. Often in the battles we face, our physical, emotional, and spiritual energy becomes depleted, and that's the beauty of Melchizedek's ministry to Abraham in supplying food, drink, and spiritual comfort.

Jesus Christ does the same for us as our "spring of living water" (John 4:14) and "bread of life," leaving us "the Comforter" to minister to our needs (John 4:14; John 6:35; John 14:26). As the better King-Priest, He is also our Father (John 10:30).

Whether you have earthly parents or can claim like Melchizedek that you are without father, mother, or genealogy, you do have a Heavenly Father that not only provides life, but an abundant life. You may not be a king, but you can live as a child of the King. You may not have a father, but you have access to the Heavenly Father. You can be a mirror image of your Father here on Earth, allowing the Holy Spirit to comfort you and generously serve others.

FOOLISH FOLLIES

A proverb in the mouth of a fool is like a stick with thorns, brandished by the hand of a drunkard. The one who hires a fool or who hires those passing by is like an archer who wounds everyone. As a dog returns to its vomit, so a fool repeats his foolishness. Do you see a man who is wise in his own eyes? There is more hope for a fool than for him.

Proverbs 26:9-12

I once knew a man who would be labelled a "fool" by all who came into contact with him. When he opened his mouth, his foolishness was revealed through vulgar language, pedantic jocularity, arrogant boasting, and thoughtless prattling of knowledge, embarrassing his wife and children regularly. He was also known for being stubborn and somewhat corrupt, not always being fair and just in his business dealings. In fact, I was never quite comfortable when we were at the same places together. I felt like God was giving me a real-life lesson on "what not to be" when I grew up.

It's in this memory a Sunday school lesson comes to my mind. My teacher, Elwin, was teaching our junior high class about King David. One particular Sunday morning, our lesson began in 1 Samuel 25 where we were introduced to a foolish man named Nabal. It's ironic that

Nabal's name reflected his foolishness, and, in verse 3, his Biblical epitaph was "harsh and evil in his dealings."

During David's traveling through the Wilderness of Paran, he and his men came across Nabal's shepherds to his 3,000 sheep and 1,000 goats. Offering protection to the men and the livestock, David made certain that no harm came to any of them. News came to David that the owner of these sheep was shearing his sheep, a massive undertaking for such a large herd. David sends ten of his young men to meet up with Nabal, telling him of the protection that had been offered and asking to take part in the feast day that normally occurred after the shearing, hoping that Nabal would feed David and his men.

As Nabal's description ran true, he foolishly and brutishly responded with insulting disregard for who David was and arrogantly accused David of being cowardly in running away from Saul. At this point, we can almost hear the Western slang, "Now them's fightin' words, Mister!" Cue the music from your favorite Western, and you've got a good idea what's going to happen. David gathers 400 of his 600 men to execute vengeance on this foolish man and his people. They began to march in on Nabal's property, fully armed and ready for battle.

Meanwhile, back at the corral, was an intelligent and beautiful woman named Abigail, wife of Nabal. The servants run to her and tell her of their master's response to David, even stating to their master's wife, "He is such a worthless fool nobody can talk to him!"

(v. 17). It seems by their confidence to tell her what happened and what they think, that they probably came to Abigail on other occasions. His poor judgment preceded him, and Abigail was going to step in and make amends to King David.

This story is one of the most riveting dramas played out in the Bible! It leaves you on the edge of your seat as you watch the drama unfold. Abigail rushed to get provisions for David and his men, bowed before him and asked that the fault be laid at her feet. Nabal got drunk and passed out, not even knowing his very life was in danger. Abigail is blessed by David as he praised God that he was prevented from vengeance by her discernment. Abigail told Nabal when he woke up what transpired while he was oblivious in his drunken stupor. Nabal had some sort of stroke or seizure and was paralyzed, and in ten days he was dead. King David takes Abigail as his wife. The End.

What a soap opera of foolish folly and veritable vengeance that was overshadowed by godly guidance and powerful protection. It's clear to say that the way of the foolish brings death and destruction, while the way of the wise brings life and health to those who seek it and practice it.

King David allowed his anger to precipitate an attack on Nabal, not consulting the Lord on how He wanted David to proceed. Had he run ahead of God in this way, David would have committed murder, damaging his character, and potentially ruining his opportunity to be King. The Lord used Abigail's humility and wisdom to prevent David from executing vengeance against Nabal and all who served him.

The Lord reminds us in Romans 12:19, "Friends, do not avenge yourselves; instead, leave room for His wrath. For it is written: Vengeance belongs to Me; I will repay, says the Lord." Abigail's speech toward King David, full of faith and devotion to God, focused on how the Lord would use him as King of Israel.

It is very probable that her marriage to Nabal was a pre-arranged marriage, and one that was very evidently ill-suited, but Abigail didn't allow her foolish husband to sway her in her firm faith walk with the God of Israel. She humbly submitted herself before the pending King David, offered him an apology, supplied him with rations for all his men, and requested only one thing from him. Abigail asked to be remembered when King David came to his throne.

King David accepted the offering, blessed Abigail's counsel and reproof, and admitted that he had been wrong. When we act on our human reasoning and emotions, we run the risk of falling into folly, acting foolishly. When we receive wise and godly counsel, humbling ourselves in reproof and correction, seeking God's wisdom in situations, we save ourselves from brutish, harsh, and foolish behavior.

Let the righteous one strike me—
it is an act of faithful love;
let him rebuke me—
it is oil for my head;
let me[a] not refuse it.
Even now my prayer is against
the evil acts of the wicked.
Psalm 141:5

PIG SLOP AND A ROYAL ROBE

Then he went to work for one of the citizens of that country, who sent him into his fields to feed pigs. He longed to eat his fill from the carob pods the pigs were eating, but no one would give him any. When he came to his senses, he said, "How many of my father's hired hands have more than enough food, and here I am dying of hunger! I'll get up, go to my father, and say to him, Father, I have sinned against heaven and in your sight. I'm no longer worthy to be called your son. Make me like one of your hired hands." So he got up and went to his father. But while the son was still a long way off, his father saw him and was filled with compassion. He ran, threw his arms around his neck, and kissed him. The son said to him, "Father, I have sinned against heaven and in your sight. I'm no longer worthy to be called your son." But the father told his slaves, "Quick! Bring out the best robe and put it on him; put a ring on his finger and sandals on his feet. Then bring the fattened calf and slaughter it, and let's celebrate with a feast, because this son of mine was dead and is alive again; he was lost and is found!" So they began to celebrate.

Luke 15:15-24

Can you picture this incredibly heart stirring scene? A wayward son, destitute and demoralized, abject in his humiliation as he came to the end of himself, his pride, and his self-sufficiency, to return home and admit defeat and prepare to beg for forgiveness. He's stinky and smelly after working with the hogs, an abomination to the Jewish culture.

His brief insanity has now brought him to a point of repentance. The sin that had consumed him had faded to a shameful end. When he became disgusted with his life, his choices, and the ultimate consequences, he decided to appeal to his father to allow him to be a servant. Even his father's servants were treated better than his current situation, and, just maybe, his father would take pity on his situation and hire him.

The broken fellowship of this family is poignant and sharp. The son, who went out to "find himself," actually lost himself. It tore the family apart. His actions brought dishonor to his father and family.

Meanwhile, back at the farm, the father prays and waits. He prays for his wayward son. He waits for his return. He is actively waiting. It sounds like a paradox, actively waiting, but the father is watching and waiting for the return of the son he loves. This father, who is so good to his servants, scans the horizon for any sign of his returning son.

There in the distance, a dejected young man walks. Suddenly, his father takes off and begins to run to him. Just the thought of this incredible display of love makes me weep. Jewish men did not run. Why did this father run, then? He ran to his son because of his obvious love for this child, and he was eager with desire to show that love to the one he'd been wronged by, to offer forgiveness and grace to this young man whom his heart loved.

Even though this young man had brought disgrace to his family. And, according to Deuteronomy 21:18-21, he should have been stoned by the neighbors, his father embraced his son, thus protecting him from a stoning. What a beautiful picture of grace.

Notice in these verses, the son isn't even able to utter his full apology and ask for forgiveness. His father steps in, interrupts him, and declares a celebration for his son "who was dead is alive again; he was lost and is found!" I find the exclamation point highly significant in the expression of rejoicing. This father was so delighted his son had returned he was joyous in his declaration of an immediate celebration.

As you continue reading through this passage, you will read that the father places a ring on his son's finger, signifying his sonship and drapes "the best robe" around his son's slumped shoulders. Possibly the father's own robe, expressing the acceptance he had for his son, welcoming him back to the family. This celebratory feast was a beautiful display of the father's joy at his son's return. No recriminations, no judgment, no shame, just forgiveness and grace, a gift that our Heavenly Father offers each one of us when we come to Him through faith in our Lord Jesus Christ.

There is so much more to this story as it is played out before an awestruck audience. What they've seen is unheard of, and yet the prodigal son has been forgiven and welcomed into the embrace of not just his father, but the rest of the household as well.

Enter the older brother. Upon hearing the raucous celebration, he asks a servant what is happening. His younger, wasteful brother has returned. His blood begins to boil and anger festers to the surface.

While there are many things that the older brother can be commended for, like obedience to his father, diligence in his work, and working hard at what he did for his father, his attitude revealed his heart's true condition. As Jesus is telling this parable to the scribes and the Pharisees, He again is reminding them that it's not what is on the outside that reveals a person's true character, it's what is in the heart.

The older brother is angry and prideful in his obedience to his father, again, doing the will of the father but not feeling it with his heart. His inward attitude was self-righteous, not seeing his own sins, but only the sins of others. In his pride and self-righteousness, he refused to forgive his brother, even when his father came out from the celebration to bring him in to see his younger brother, he stayed outside of the tent of celebration and pouted.

When we are out of fellowship with God, the fellowship with our brothers and sisters is broken. When we harbor unforgiveness in our heart, we cannot have communion with God (Matthew 5:21-26). If our brothers and sisters show true repentance, we are commanded by Jesus to forgive those who have sinned and extend to them restoration with grace and humility.

Although we don't know the ending to the parable, we do see that the father has the last word. The father not only showed love to his returning prodigal child but showed the same love to his older son. One accepted his love, the other rejected it. One humbled himself, the other lifted himself up in pride. Two sons, one father...a Father like mine.

Reflection

Which son are you? The one who has come to the end of himself or the one full of pride?

How would repentance of the sin of pride free you from its bondage and allow you to rejoice in the love of the Father?

There is joy in a forgiving spirit. Who do you need to forgive? Of whom do you need to ask for forgiveness?

I DON'T DESERVE THIS

But even if you should suffer for righteousness, you are blessed. Do not fear what they fear or be disturbed but honor the Messiah as Lord in your hearts. Always be ready to give a defense to anyone who asks you for a reason for the hope that is in you. However, do this with gentleness and respect, keeping your conscience clear, so that when you are accused, those who denounce your Christian life will be put to shame. For it is better to suffer for doing good, if that should be God's will, than for doing evil.

1 Peter 3:14-17

I was a senior in high school in a public speaking class. The assignment was to speak on something that was a highly controversial subject. I choose to speak on a religious cult that was prevalent in my town. I researched diligently and prepared my speech to the point of memorization. I was terribly nervous. The preceding year, I had spoken on another controversial subject and had been harassed and jeered at for several weeks before the uproar died down. As far as I knew, I was the only Christian in my class. The religious cult held a large population in our community, and I was already an "outsider" since I moved there just a couple years prior.

Prayed up and ready to stand before my class, I handed my teacher the prepared speech and stepped up to the podium. Before I even opened my mouth, she yelled at me to leave her classroom and go immediately to the principal's office where I would be "dealt with." I tried to defend my position, but this just infuriated her to the point of screaming at me.

I walked the long hallway to the principal's office, praying all the way that whatever God was leading me to do, that He would give me wisdom and words in the moment. After an intense afternoon of having my parents called in to meet with the principal and myself, the ultimatum was handed down. Either I conform to the classroom and redo my work on a less controversial subject (what's the point of a choosing controversial subject anyway?) or take a zero on the assignment and be excluded from class for a week. All eyes were on me. Do I stand up for what I believe to be the truth or back down and hide what God had clearly prepared me to do?

It was in those brief moments, I called out for wisdom... and God granted me what I needed in that situation. I took a zero on the assignment, but, because of the raucous it caused, I was able to share with more people than just the thirty individuals in my class the lies of the cult. I was being stopped by students who were curious. I was asked by teachers who had heard about the "situation I caused" in the classroom. The principal asked intelligent questions about my research and even read my paper.

I truly was inadequate for the job God asked me to do, but, because I trusted Him at His word, I was given the wisdom needed for the moment. God has promised us in Matthew 10:19, "But when they hand you over, don't worry about how or what you should speak. For you will be given what to say at that hour."

God has called us to serve Him, even when we experience undeserved suffering or persecution. When we do what is right and good and suffer for it, we can count it a privilege to suffer as it pleases God. Hebrews 11's Hall of Faith is full of men and women who suffered for doing what is right and good.

The world's harsh treatment, family or friends scoffing, lack of formal education, etc., tempts us to withdraw and refuse to expose our lack of wisdom for fear of being shamed by others, but God gives generously, without criticizing anyone who asks. Remember Solomon, when asked by God in 1 Kings 3:1-15 what Solomon would desire above anything and God would give it to him? What was Solomon's response? Solomon responded in a request for wisdom: an obedient, discernment, and wise heart. Solomon knew that his request for wisdom was going to have to be an action of obedience, and he asked for it.

The Apostle Paul had many opportunities to speak before men, sharing the gospel of Jesus Christ to government officials. God always gave him the words to say with boldness. As a child, I remember being taught about the time that Paul was brought in before Festus and King Agrippa in Acts 26:24-32. I was amazed at

Paul's brazen confidence as he stood before these two men and quite possibly many more as he tried to persuade them to follow Christ. In that moment, God gave Paul the words to speak, and men heard life changing news during Paul's defense of himself as a minister of the Gospel of Christ.

As we stand in reverence of God's Word, may we "always be ready to give a defense to anyone who asks you for a reason for the hope that is in you." If we suffer for Christ, it is an honor. Live in such a way that there is no question that you are a Christian, responding to the world with gentleness and respect so that your accusers will be put to shame if you are suffering for doing good and God's will.

Reflection

Have you experienced suffering while doing good for the will of God?

Did you respond with gentleness and respect or in anger at your accusers?

How does Paul's example before King Agrippa or Jesus' response to His accusers before His crucifixion help you as you respond?

A FAITH WALK ON ROUGH ROADS

Consider it a great joy, my brothers, whenever you experience various trials, knowing that the testing of your faith produces endurance. But endurance must do its complete work, so that you may be mature and complete lacking nothing.

James 1:2-4

I was twelve years old when God used a particularly difficult summer to begin shaping me in my faith walk and growth. That summer, my mom was in a swimming accident that nearly broke her neck. She was only thirty-three years old. This left her in traction for six weeks with many years of rehabilitation to follow. Doctors said she would never use her arms again, but by the grace of God, she regained full use of her arms; however, she lived the remainder of her life with chronic neck and back pain.

During my mom's recovery, I often stayed with my grandparents on their farm. It was a magical place to be, and I loved every moment there. My grandpa raised horses, so one of my favorite things to do was go horseback riding. Grandpa had set me up with a horse in the corral with strict instructions just to walk Rusty in circles. My memory is a little vague at this point whether I intentionally kicked Rusty in the flanks or not, but my last cognitive memory was being thrown over Rusty's head, waking up to seeing my grandma's face over my own. Although, my biggest concern was finding my glasses in the tall grass!

After a horrendous nine mile drive over gravel roads to the nearest hospital, it was revealed that my left wrist and left shoulder were broken. The highlight of that event was that the ER staff were impressed by my polished nails done like candy canes (don't ask me why that's one of the only things I can remember). It must have made everything better, though, because I don't have many memories after that for a while! I guess it doesn't matter what was wrong as long as you look good!

Later that fall, my family went out to a local farm that had a tree grove with plenty of deadwood to cut firewood for the winter. My brothers and I played in and amongst the underbrush while Mom and Dad prepared to cut down a dead tree. Once everything was ready, we kids got into the truck bed to be out of the way. Chainsaw in hand, my dad began to carefully cut down the tree. Mom stood off to the side to give plenty of room for the tree to fall. Suddenly, without warning, the tree swung in a completely different direction, tangling my dad in the underbrush and crushing him to the ground.

As we watched in helplessness, my mom jumped right into action and with the strength only seen in Hercules. My mom lifted the massive tree off my dad and was able to get him to the pickup truck bed. He was badly injured, and his breathing was labored. Slowly, we began the painfully long trek down out of the wooded area, through the hilly cattle farmland, through a gate and was within a half mile of the paved highway when a neighbor friend showed up.

He and my mom began to unhook the wood trailer from the truck, but again, in a freak accident, the tongue of the wood trailer caught my mom's leg and sent her sprawling, reinjuring her back and neck. The friend left and raced ahead to call for emergency help. After what seemed like years, we made it to my other grandparent's farm where the ambulance was waiting for us, ready to transport my dad to the hospital where he was diagnosed with three broken ribs, a broken knee, and multiple contusions and abrasions, not to mention a complete body sprain (I mean, when you wrestle with trees, expect to get hurt!).

I share these trials with you because, while I didn't see it or understand it at the time, God was already at work shaping my heart and stretching my faith. These trials were teaching my family and me the power of our faith in the process of endurance. Endurance means the power of enduring a difficult process without giving way. Our faith and complete trust in the Lord were now being shaped in our lives, helping us to endure the trials we faced.

Although we didn't always comprehend why we were experiencing these difficulties, I clung to another verse that had become precious to me in my middle school years. Proverbs 3:5-6 says, "Trust in the Lord with all your heart and lean not on your own under-standing. In all your ways acknowledge Him and He will direct your paths." Even when the struggle was real to trust God's hands, I could trust His heart.

In your most recent trial, do you see the pattern of faith, endurance, maturity, and completeness? If not, perhaps God is chastening you, convicting you of your need to get things right with Him. Ask God to show you if He is shaping you in your faith walk, or if God is allowing a trial to enter our life to convict you of a sin that He wants you to confess to Him.

Personally, God has convicted me of my own self-reliance (I've got this!), pride (I deserve better!), anger (Why does this stuff always happen to me?), and critical spirit (Well, they certainly got what they deserved!). It's in those trials that God reveals Himself to me, and I humbly come before Him asking for for-giveness. We can, like the psalmist of Psalm 139:23-24, pray, "Search me, God, and know my heart; test me and know my concerns. See if there is any offensive way in me: lead me in the everlasting way."

In stretching us or convicting us, James reminds us that it is in these trials that God is shaping us, our faith producing endurance and steadfastness through which is our basis (and promise) that we will find joy. As we persevere through increasing levels of suffer-ing, we will become patient in the process, knowing that God is continuing to work, producing in us spiri-tual maturity that glorifies God and offers hope to the world around us.

Reflection

Are you in a time of trial that is crushing you right now? How are you responding? In anger or humility?

Can you trust God even if the outcome isn't what you want?

How can you merge the idea of finding joy even as you face trials?

I WILL ALWAYS REMEMBER YOU

Cornelius replied, "Four days ago at this hour, at three in the afternoon, I was praying in my house. Just then a man in a dazzling robe stood before me and said, 'Cornelius, your prayer has been heard, and your acts of charity have been remembered in God's sight...'"

Acts 10:30-31

There she was. No longer the little girl I remember, but older, she was now almost eight years old. I hadn't seen her in over a year and know that children tend to forget people who move away when they are young. But she remembered me. Arms outstretched, she hugged me with all of her might. "Are you Miss Amy Jo?" she smiled up at me. I replied, "Yes, I am, Allie!" Tears choked me full of nostalgia for the people I had loved and served in my previous church of fifteen years. Moving two hours away seemed like two states away. Children that I had taught and ministered to had grown up, gotten taller, and remembered.

I was speaking at the church's junior's camp this week, and Allie's older sister, Evie, was going to be there as a camper. Allie, visiting her Grandma who was also the camp nurse, decided to hang out with me for the afternoon as we waited for campers to arrive. Putting her little hand in my hand, we ran across the open expanse of the camp, walked the gravel pathways, played on the jungle gym equipment, and finally took time to rest in the shade of a majestic oak tree that boasted a tire swing. It was there that Allie began to really share with me.

"I will always remember you," she began as she giggled when the swing took her higher.

"Oh yeah? What do you remember about me?" I enquired.

"Well, I remember your teeth and those earrings. You always wore those kinds of earrings."

"Hoops? Yep, I like wearing hoop earrings. What else do you remember?"

"I remember your hair is always so blond and your glasses. And your face is always smiling. I remember your Mom died."

"Yes, she did die, but you came to the visitation and gave me a big hug that made me feel better." Getting choked up again, I fought the tears of remembering how healing her little hug had been at such a difficult time in my life.

"I will always remember you on stage singing and teaching. You did funny crazy things." Allie continued. "I wish you hadn't gone away."

I stopped asking questions and started to ponder these childlike statements in my heart. I hadn't wanted to leave, but God had clearly given our family direction it was time to move. My constant prayer at the time of children's ministry was that these children God had allowed to be in my care would come to know and follow Jesus, but even more than that. I prayed they would grow in the love of Jesus and, one day, they would themselves be ministers of the Gospel of Christ through children's ministry, VBS, and Sunday school teaching.

Her statement brought to my mind the story of Cornelius in the New Testament book of Acts. Cornelius, a Gentile centurion, upright and God-fearing had a divine appointment with the Apostle Peter. Through a series of events, Peter visited Cornelius in his home after God gave Peter a vision regarding the message of salvation was now available to the Gentile nations. Even before Peter entered Cornelius's house, Cornelius's prayers had been heard by God. All that Cornelius did to honor of God was remembered.

The childlike openness of Cornelius and his desire for his close family and friends to experience this visit from Peter gave way to something bigger than Cornelius could even imagine. It was the opening of the message that God's gift of salvation was for all mankind, no matter their ethnic situation or cultural background.

God was using Jesus's disciples to go into all the world as bold witnesses calling the unbelievers to a saving faith. Everything that Cornelius had done previously, preparing his family and friends, and, I dare say, even his soldiers that were under his command to be ready and receptive to the gospel of Jesus Christ.

"Your acts of charity have been remembered..." Love put to action is charity. Cornelius lived out his life honoring God by being charitable to those he was around. God remembered him and what he did. Touching lives, planting seeds, and sharing the love of God with others.

Reflection

What will you be remembered for doing to further the gospel of Christ?

Can you think of individuals who have touched your life, bringing you into a closer walk with God?

Are you charitable towards others? Share some practical ways you can pray for others and act on the charity God has called you to do.

ON A HILL

No one has ascended into Heaven except the One who descended from Heaven—the Son of Man. Just as Moses lifted up the snake in the wilderness, so the Son of Man must be lifted up, so that everyone who believes in Him will have eternal life.

John 3:13-15

Walking through the church camp this morning in the early dawn moments, the sun fragmenting through the leafy green trees, I breathed in deeply the scents of summer. Reaching the top of the hill always brings such a strong emotional response as three crosses line the horizon, reminding me of why I am here. This year, I'm the speaker to junior campers, ages eight to eleven, but previous years I had served alongside my husband as the camp nurse (I'm the one who brought treats while my husband treated injuries of all kinds), while I also volunteered as gardener, maintenance helper, and camp store clerk.

No matter the reason for me being here at this camp, my trek to the top of the hill is a time of readjusting my heart and mind on Jesus. I stand there at the top and stare at the crosses heavy with the morning dew, and, in my imaginative speculation, wonder about the cross that held my Savior. Had it brought the same introspective contemplation from the men and women who witnessed the "lifting up of the Son of Man"?

In Numbers 21:4-9, the children of Israel became impatient because of their long journey through the wilderness. They grumbled and complained so much that the LORD sent poisonous snakes as a punishment for their sin against Himself and their leader, Moses. Realizing their sin, they begged Moses to intercede on their behalf to the LORD asking for deliverance, yet again. Moses immediately went to the LORD asking for deliverance from the poisonous snakes.

Moses was instructed to make a bronze snake on top of a pole. Anyone who is bitten would be able to look at the bronze snake, recover, and live. God's antidote was faith in His provision of healing, not in the snake as an idol. There was one other time that God provided an antidote to sin.

Jesus was lifted up on a cross as the deliverance from the disease of sin and eternal death. The Son of Man was nailed to a cruel cross high on the hill so that all could see. Jesus carried His own cross to the Skull Place, called Golgotha, in Latin meaning "Calvary." He was "high and lifted up" for our sins. Continuing on in this chapter, many of the Jews saw Him because He was near the city at the time of Passover. The final sacrifice offered by the perfect Lamb of God to take away the sins of the world. Once and for all. No other sacrifice had to be made to cover the sins of mankind. Jesus finished the work at the cross. In His resurrection, He defeated death. He willingly laid down His life to offer a way to bring together a Righteous and Holy God with a sinful people.

The sacrifice of Jesus paid for the sins of the world, and the work of the gospel continues as we share this complete act of *agape* love with a world that desperately needs Him. "For God loved the world in this way: He gave His One and Only Son, so that everyone who believes in Him will not perish but have eternal life" (John 3:16).

It was finished on a hill
The Lord, He died for me
A sacrifice that lingers still
Upon that rugged tree

Oh Lord, my sins you have paid
The ultimate sacrifice
In that moment, Death was stayed
For You bestowed eternal life

The empty cross, the empty grave
You are no longer there
You came to seek and save
The lost from everywhere

Not to perish in this life we live
To share the gospel story
The message that salvation gives
Bringing Him new souls to glory

GETTING REAL WITH GOD

Instead, if you really change your ways and your actions, if you act justly toward one another, if you no longer oppress the foreigner, the fatherless, and the widow and no longer shed innocent blood in this place or follow other gods, bringing harm on yourselves, I will allow you to live in this place, the land I gave to your ancestors long ago and forever.

Jeremiah 7:5-7

"Saying you're sorry means that you won't do that ever again" was a phrase I remember hearing in my formative years. It usually followed getting caught at doing something I wasn't supposed to do or not doing something I was supposed to do. I've always felt the need to apologize. Whether the guilt is actually mine or not doesn't matter. If the sun is shining and someone wants rain, you will find me saying "I'm sorry." If the rain is beating down and someone wants sun, the same phrase will be uttered.

There were many times that my apology was given just to be given. It had no depth to it, no real meaning or value. It "got me off the hook" instead of being in trouble. It wasn't until I was in high school when the weight of my sin caused me to "get real with God" and my parents. Although, before my sin was brought to my attention, I didn't see it as "really bad" or anything I needed to seek forgiveness for in my life. My relationship with my parents and God seemed to be shallow and ineffectual.

After this particularly "educational moment," I felt my heart break that I not only let my parents down, hurting them deeply, but that I disappointed God with my behavior, causing others to stumble and fall. In that instance, I came face to face with my sin and with God. Up to this point, I had been paying lip service to God, but my heart was divided, worshipping at the feet of "Me."

Jeremiah has been in my metaphorical book of "Bible Super Heroes" because of his tenacity to bring a message of God's judgment to a people who were unresponsive. Jeremiah loved God's Word so much that he is known for being a prophet of "the word of the LORD" (1:2). In fact, Jeremiah declared that God's words were joy and food for his soul (15:16). Jeremiah was a devoted prophet to the LORD God of Israel, but his ministry was a burden as he repeatedly brought warnings to these spiritual bankrupt people.

As you read through the book of Jeremiah, you find that the people of Judah were a people of divided hearts—worshipping God with their words, but committing idolatry with temple idols such as Baal, Ashtoreth, Chemosh and other gods and goddesses of the heathen nations surrounding them. They conveniently forgot the Ten Commandments in lieu of the lust of their own flesh.

Jeremiah exposed these sins, and it almost cost him his life. Not only were they practicing idolatry, but they were abusing and misusing their brothers and sisters. The court system and judges practiced corruption. The weak and defenseless in society were treated badly or were murdered. Judah's testimony was full of deliberate sinfulness and rebellion.

But God, in His great mercy, offered them blessing and protection if they would just "get real with Him," repent of their sins, and begin to live in a way that would bring honor and glory to the God of Israel. God cares how His people treat the weak and defenseless (James 1:27). God wants His people's actions and words in true repentance to set in motion the promises God has made them. He wants the honest judgment of His people in courtrooms and in their business dealings.

It sounds like Jeremiah is describing the time we are walking through today. The injustice, prejudice, and worship of idols is very much present in our world. Looking at the Ten Commandments, we see how these are broken constantly in social media, news media, and even within the Christian community. Let the weight of our sin bring us to our knees at the feet of Jesus. May we continue to examine our lives in light of a Holy God. May we change our ways and our actions so that we can claim God's promises of a life of abundant blessings in our obedience to Him.

Reflection

Ask God to show you areas that you need repentance. Take your time to be still and sit with Him. Write down where He wants you to confess and repent.

Are you practicing justice and integrity to others? In what ways could you improve?

James 1:27 says that "pure and undefiled religion before our God and Father is this: to look after orphans and widows in their distress and to keep oneself unstained by the world." How does this mirror your daily practice?

DEATH OF SELF-SUFFICIENCY

Now this is what the LORD says—the One who created you, Jacob, and the One who formed you, Israel—"Do not fear, for I have redeemed you; I have called you by your name; you are Mine. I will be with you when you pass through the waters, and when you pass through the rivers, they will not overwhelm you. You will not be scorched when you walk through the fire, and the flame will not burn you. For I Yahweh your God, the Holy One of Israel, and your Savior, give Egypt as a ransom for you, Cush and Seba in your place."

Isaiah 43:1-3

Do you remember the Sunday school song "The wise man built his house upon the rock"? Well, in the summer of 2018, this song began to ring through my head as we faced one of the most devastating storms central Iowa had seen in over twenty years. A knock at our apartment door was the first indication that our life was going to be completely disrupted for quite a while. Water was bubbling up through the hallway drain, coming up through the toilets, the faucets in the tub, and was actually running down the stairs from the flooded parking lot.

My husband and I tried to stem the flow of water, but it was hopeless. The water kept coming, and finally at 10:30pm, we were taken to temporary shelter. That night, tears ran down my face, and my heart felt like it was literally breaking. I didn't know how much more I could take. We were facing many challenges in our lives, and this was the straw breaking the proverbial camel's back. But God knew, and it was this assurance that gave me the strength to get out of bed the next morning.

Getting in the shower, I began questioning God and even silently expressing my displeasure at the current circumstances. I don't know about you, but sometimes when my head and heart don't match, God has to figuratively "knock me upside the head," in love of course. Stepping into the hot water, I looked up at the water, only to have the entire shower head fall off and bop me on the forehead. I started to cry and then to laugh because of the irony. One might say that there were "showers of blessings" that would be forthcoming.

After working for many hours the following day to salvage what we could, my husband said we needed some waterproof containers. Standing in front of the empty shelves at Walmart, I started to crumble. Emotionally exhausted, I mentally snapped, and I wept in frustration and weariness. Even as I cried silently, I prayed again more fervently. It was at this point that God again proved Himself to be the faithful, reliable Shepherd of His children. As I walked around the corner, ready to leave without what we came for, a voice beside me said, "We are so glad to see you! We heard what happened, and we were going to call you as soon as we got home. But we decided you have to come live in our home for the next six weeks!"

That night found our family falling literally exhausted into bed, praying, and me trying to figure out what to do the next day. I remember a godly woman telling me once, "When you don't know what to do, do the next thing." That night I lay awake most of the night praying, crying, and trying to make sense of this season of trials. The next morning, we woke early and trudged back to the apartment to continue cleaning. As we entered the building, the smell hit us like a cesspool of mold, rotten food, and wet carpet. We began to cry as we opened our apartment door. The water had subsided, but what we saw just left us disheartened.

Later in the day, a friend stopped by with an envelope of money to help with whatever expenses we would be incurring that week. He told us he would be praying for us and to please allow God to minister through him as we had needs.

God had miraculously provided a place for us to live rent free for the time we needed to find a new home. God had given us financial resources to use for our needs. Our Keystone Church family had come together and provided a bag full of gift cards for restaurants, stores, gas stations, as well as handwritten notes of encouragement from people who didn't know us and who we didn't know. It was overwhelming. God was continuing to prove Himself to be faithful in this season of trials.

I began to call my experience the "*death of self-sufficiency.*" I was reminded so much of Moses, Peter, and Sarah as, in their own way, they tried to control or manipulate circumstances in their own strength and messed up big time. At one time, I would have boasted in my accomplished self-sufficiency, but you see, this isn't where God wants us to be in our dependence on Him during trials or even when we are not facing trials.

We had been living in our temporary housing for a couple of weeks. This should have been a time of joy and relief of God's hand of provision for us, however, I was disagreeable, frustrated, and fearful about our future. Even as I prayed for God to "fix things", I would immediately set about trying to manipulate circumstances to fit into what I thought were the correct solutions to our dilemma. I was teaching a summer Bible study, in the Word daily and praying, but my time with God seemed to be forced. As I would spend fruitless hours trying to "fix everything," I realized that I was just spinning my wheels and not getting anywhere. Manipulating God doesn't work, but God will allow us to exhaust ourselves until we are ready to lean on Him in complete trust.

That particular morning started as usual. I got up and grabbed my Bible. Sitting on the deck in the morning sun, I began to read and study. God began to reveal to me some areas I wasn't giving fully to Him, I was still controlling. Daily I would attempt to draw attention to our house that had been for sale for almost two years either on social media or talk about it to anyone who would listen. Because we had been paying rent and a mortgage, our finances were in terrible shape, but I was still trying to make ends meet with very little success, which caused disruptions in my marriage from the pressure I was placing on my already hard-working husband. One thing led to another, and I started to get defensive with God, justifying and rationalizing my actions and responses. The more I argued with God, the more convicted I became, and it wasn't long before I slammed my Bible shut.

Sensing that nothing good was going to continue, I decided to get in the shower. In the shower, I began to cry. I mean ugly cry. I began to cry out to Heavenly Father that I was at the end of myself. I literally fell to my knees and cried out in desperation. I couldn't do this on my own anymore. I didn't have anything left. I cried until there was nothing left. I confessed my pride and self-sufficiency, my pride *in* my self-sufficiency, emptying myself completely and asking my Heavenly Father to intervene. Calmed by the Holy Spirit, I began to feel a calmness and peace that infused my heart and mind.

Just as in these verses above, God was calling my name, reminding me that He had redeemed me, and I am His. It didn't matter what I was facing, Yahweh my God was with me, and He wasn't leaving me on my own. It wasn't up to me to "figure it out." I didn't have to do this on my own. God uses the storms of life (even showers of blessings) to remind me that I don't need to fear because He is with me through it all. You and I can fully rely on the sufficiency of the Holy One of Israel, our Savior and Creator.

Reflection

Are you living in self-sufficiency, controlling and manip-ulating the plan of God to fit into what you think is best?

How can you relinquish control and allow God to lead you through life?

Have you been through the "death of self-sufficiency"? What lessons did God teach you through your experience?

DRIED RASPBERRIES

The Brother of humble circumstances should boast in his exaltation, but the one who is rich should boast in his humiliation because he will pass away like a flower of the field. For the sun rises with its scorching heat and dries up the grass; its flower falls off and its beautiful appearance is destroyed. In the same way, the rich man will wither away while pursuing his activities.

James 1:9-11

In our early married years, we struggled financially, oftentimes not having enough to buy adequate groceries or fill up our gas tank. My husband had just finished nursing school, and we had relocated to a small community several states away from our family and friends with little more than the clothes on our backs. Taking on extra jobs to help ends meet, I began to clean the house of a wealthy family.

The first time I drove up the winding long driveway edged with a white picket fence, I was in awe of stepping foot into this mansion that I'd only seen from the road. The massive brick structure and its white pillars gave an air of money and affluence, almost to the point of excess. To complete the picture, the house-keeper greeted me at the door and gave me a tour of the house and grounds. I noticed several others working the property, some mowing the vast yards, some working in the barns, and others doing maintenance around the property.

There was luxurious carpeting, priceless artwork, and marble countertops. Chandeliers adorned main rooms, even the master bathroom. I remember gazing open mouthed at the opulence of the many possessions that decorated the house. In the four-car garage were vehicles with names I'd only read about in books. A couple of the cars were covered with dust covers and were only driven one or two times a year. One of the classic cars was worth more than the little house we were living in!

I asked the housekeeper, who had worked for this family for years, "Would you rather have this life of luxury or are you happy just being a housekeeper?" She paused before answering me. "Honestly, I wouldn't want what she has. She spent the early part of her life worrying about where the money was going to come from, and, after inheriting it, she worries constantly about how to keep it all. She also worries about who her true friends are. Even her family tries to get at her money. She trusts very few people. It's not a peaceful life. I'm content to clean her home, enjoy the fruits of her labor and go home at night to my modest home."

James reminds us that as we are going through life, whether poor or rich, we have nothing in ourselves to boast of. We both equally share in life here on Earth and ultimately in death. When I finally did meet the owner, I was amazed by her generosity to certain charity groups, acting as a chairperson for a couple of them. However, I noticed that she seemed to be stingy with her own workers, expecting and demanding perfection from them with minimal pay and very little encouragement.

One day after I began working for her, I was asked to pick raspberries in the afternoon heat. Summers in Iowa are notoriously hot and humid. That day the temperature was in the upper nineties, and the raspberry bushes held no shade. For three hours I picked raspberries, incurring a sunburn on my blond head and multiple scratches and scrapes from the raspberry bushes.

You can then understand my angry tears, for the very next morning when I showed up to work, I was chastised. "Did you pick the raspberries?" the owner asked me, and upon my affirmation, she continued. "These raspberries were for my Mama. There were some dried ones in the batch, so I threw them all out. Next time make sure you only pick good ones." Now from where I come from, raspberries are a valuable commodity and would *never* be thrown out. It would have been a simple task to sort through and remove the dried berries.

I learned much from this wealthy woman. I learned how to be grateful for God's daily benefits, for abundant blessings when they came, and show appreciation to others for gifts given to our family by others who had little to nothing as well. I also learned how important it is to be fair and honest in all my business dealings. God is fully aware of how we treat others, whether they are employees or not. I have become ever aware that those who humble themselves to do menial jobs at my request need to be treated with respect.

James also warns us against favoritism, being a fair and honest employer as well as a hard-working employee in chapters 2 and 4. The warning to those who are rich and unfairly treat their workers comes in chapter 5. Throughout the book of James, the author continuously reminds us that God the Father is aware of how we treat others, whether as a worker ourselves, or as the boss. God sees the helplessness of the needy, but also the unjust treatment from the wealthy.

It is by our treatment of one another as Children of God that others see Christ reflected in our lives. How beautiful it is when you are acknowledged by your work ethic, generosity of gifts and talents, treatment of others, and love for your brothers and sisters in Christ!

Although that day was a difficult day for me, deflating my hard work and desire to gain approval of my boss, I also gleaned much in my own personal life. I've remembered how I felt, not ever wanting someone who is working for me to experience that degradation. Even within my own family, when one of my daughters, husband, or son-in-law does something for me, I let them know how much I appreciate their help in whatever they do for me. I love to give extra tips to those people who go above and beyond at restaurants, massages, haircuts, or house cleaning.

Equal before God, we have nothing in ourselves to boast of in our poverty or in our wealth. As God has blessed you, may you in turn be a blessing to others. Be fair and honest. Be kind and don't show favoritism. Be a good worker or a good boss. "Whatever you do, do it enthusiastically, as something done for the Lord and not for men" (Colossians 3:23).

PUTTING WHEELS TO YOUR MEALS

"There's a boy here who has five barley loaves and two fish-but what are they for so many?" Then Jesus said, "Have the people sit down." There was plenty of grass in that place, so they sat down. The men numbered about 5,000. Then Jesus took the loaves, and after giving thanks He distributed them to those who were seated-so also with the fish, as much as they wanted.

John 6:9-11

I'm known in my circle of friends and family for my homemade mac 'n cheese. When people come to visit, that's often the first thing they request for a meal. It's not a difficult dish to make, but it does use some rich ingredients, takes time and careful watching so it doesn't scorch on the stovetop. Sometimes when I want to get fancy, I experiment with different kinds of cheese that will compliment whatever meat choice is made.

When I hear of a family in need, a sickness or death in a family, this is the dish that I make and deliver. My daughters have asked on occasion, "Why do you always make them mac 'n cheese?" Well, it all goes back to a difficult time in my life when someone pre-pared mac 'n cheese and shared it with me. Such a simple dish that not only fed my whole family, but it brought comfort to our souls emotionally as well as feeding us physically. Each time I share this dish with others, it's a memorial of a time in our lives when it was very much appreciated.

In John 6:4-13, we find that Jesus and the disciples have gone up into the mountains to rest and retreat. They had ministered to many sick individuals, providing healing and comfort to those in need. Then add all the activity that was taking place during this time as it was soon to be Passover. I imagine the streets were flooding with people who needed a healing touch from Jesus. So off they retreated into nature for some desperately needed "self-care."

However, because of the "hands on ministry" of Jesus, many of the crowds followed Him and the disciples up into the mountain. As Jesus looked up and saw the large number of people headed towards Him, I wondered what Jesus and the disciples thought. What were they doing? Taking naps, joking around, talking amongst themselves? Or did Jesus continue to offer instruction, continuing to feed into their hearts the ministry He would be leaving them with in the days ahead? Whatever they were doing, they were about to have their quiet time interrupted in a big way!

This huge crowd of people had walked a great distance to catch up to Jesus. Men, women, and children were determined in their pursuit, desiring to seek out the Lord. Jesus used this as an opportunity to test His disciples. He asked about providing for the crowd's physical needs, "Where will we buy bread that these people may eat?" It's here that I just melt in compassion towards Phillip. He touches my "hospitality heart" with his quiet obvious words, "Two hundred denarii worth of bread wouldn't be enough for them each to have a little." This would have been my first response. My second response would be to rummage around in the pantry trying to figure out what I could make with what little I had on hand.

Jesus continued to teach them, as He continues to teach us. He practically led them (and us) in their faith walk. A boy steps up with his lunch bag of bread and fish, handing it over to the Master Chef. It's at this point I'm convicted by his willingness to share this meager meal with everyone there, a child-like faith in a grown-up world. A common meal for the common man, just like mac 'n cheese. But the doubt in the disciples was palpable. Could Jesus feed the massive group with just some fish and bread? (Isn't it beautiful that God shows us that the disciples that walked with Jesus daily still struggled with doubt even as they believed in faith?)

All eyes were on Jesus as He gave thanks to the Lord for the provisions, the daily bread if you will, that had been offered, and began to break the pieces into baskets that were soon making their way through the crowds of hungry people (roughly 15,000 men, women, and children)...hungry for both the bread and fishes and for the Bread of Life and the Fisher of Men.

When their bellies were satisfied, Jesus commanded His disciples to collect the leftovers, filling twelve baskets. Jesus tended to the needs of those "children" God had given Him. We, too, need to tend carefully to the needs of those God brings into our world. Putting wheels to our meals, feeding both the body and the spirit, just as Jesus did.

Reflection

Thinking back over the last several weeks, has there been someone that has stepped in to provide for you with a meal, groceries, or a word needed in a time of unbelief? How did this small act affect you?

How can you practically put wheels to your meals by helping out someone in need? A bag of groceries, a gift card to a restaurant, or a piece of candy to let them know they are thought of by you?

An act of kindness, it seems to me,
Best summed up in a cup of tea.
A cookie or a piece of cake,
Blessed to give much more than take.
A gift from a friend or a stranger, indeed,
Fulfilling the heart's quiet prayerful need.

JOY IN THE LORD

The LORD is my shepherd; there is nothing I lack. He lets me lie down in green pastures, He renews my life; He leads me along the right paths for His name's sake. Even when I go through the darkest valley, I fear no danger for You are with me; Your rod and Your staff—they comfort me. You prepare a table before me in the presence of my enemies; You anoint my head with oil; my cup overflows. Only goodness and faithful love will pursue me all the days of my life, and I will dwell in the house of the LORD as long as I live.

Psalm 23

During the beginning of the COVID Pandemic of 2020, I marveled at the empty grocery shelves, hoarding of certain items, and the rampant fear that seemed to have paralyzed our country. I knew I needed to combat the rising fear and lies the news media was broadcasting in my own heart. Picking up my Bible, I turned to Psalm 23, a favorite passage of scripture to me. The beautiful depictions of the Shepherd being written about began to infuse my heart, allowing a sweet peace to wash over me.

I often reflect on the role of God as my Shepherd. King David's description of our Good Shepherd brings us absolute confidence. Several years ago, a dear friend of mine gave me a book that has become a treasure to me. It's called *A Look at Psalm 23* by W. Phillip Keller.[5] In his book, Mr. Keller, a former shepherd, clearly explains each nuance of this psalm in relation to the care given to sheep by their shepherd. I found fascinating the intricate detail the shepherd has for the day to day care of his sheep, in much the same way as the intimate detail that God has for each of us.

As I was preparing to speak at a women's event, I decided to use some humor to help alleviate the feeling of fear and panic. I started thinking back over the last few weeks of what I had personally experienced and wrote a revised edition of Psalm 23 in honor of the COVID-19 Pandemic.

> The LORD is my Shepherd, there is nothing I lack, except toilet paper, bottled water, and hand sanitizer.
>
> He lets me lie down in green pastures because I haven't washed the sheets since the beginning of our isolation;
>
> He leads me beside quiet waters as I do the umpteenth load of laundry only to have it sit in the clothes basket until someone finally decides to fold it.
>
> He renews my life by allowing new episodes to be put on some of my favorite shows on Netflix, Acorn, or Amazon Prime;
>
> He leads me along the right paths that are clearly marked with orange tape and chains in the food aisles for His name's sake.
>
> Even when I go through the darkest valley, the crowded stores of Menards, Aldi or Walmart, I fear

no danger, for You are with me when I sneeze or cough; Your rod and N-95 mask comfort me.

You prepare a table from McDonald's, Chipotle and Papa John's before me in the presence of my enemies or those people that are currently eating me out of house and home.

You anoint my head with oil when I choose to shower and wash my hair...has it been three days already? My cup and plate overflow several times a day.

Only goodness and faithful love will pursue me because with my weight gain, I couldn't run from anything else all the days of my life, which seems like an eternity of social distancing.

And I will dwell in the house with these people You have given me until the "in shelter" is lifted for as long as I live and keep my sanity.

Now obviously, I have taken great liberties with the original text, but sometimes we need to be reminded in humor of our reactions to irritations, challenges and inconveniences that crisis can produce; however, we are also reminded of the protective care and keeping of our Heavenly Father. So practically speaking, how can we find joy in our daily walk?

Joy *is not* an emotion that can be faked. Joy is a deep-down sense of emotional wellbeing, knowing that our strength comes from the Lord. Nehemiah 8:10 says, "Go and eat what is rich, drink what is sweet, and send portions to those who have nothing prepared, since today is holy to our Lord. Do not grieve, because the JOY OF THE LORD is your stronghold." Our true strength and security are found only in the Lord.

Joy *is not* dependent on our circumstances. God continues to be our protection as we remain faithful to Him no matter what we are facing. Psalm 5:11 says, "But let all who take refuge in You rejoice, let them shout for joy forever. May You shelter them and may those who love Your name boast about You." The words used here are military terms. God's protection assures us that we can take refuge in Him as He fights our battle for us.

Joy *is* being secure in the Lord. He is our stronghold, shield, and shelter. Here, the psalmist continues using military words, describing God as our "protective gear" as He battles on our behalf. Psalm 5:12 says, "For You, Lord, Bless the righteous one; You surround him with favor like a shield." The original word for shield describes a large piece of flattened metal that was placed in front of a soldier to protect his entire body. God is our shield, completely protecting us from the enemy.

Joy comes when we have an eternal view for our lives. When we see and understand Christ willingly gave Himself so that we might have eternal life, our current trials seem insignificant to the joy and hope we will have in Heaven, even being rewarded for our faithfulness to Him during our trials. James 1:12 says, "A man or woman who endures trials is blessed, because when he passes the test he will receive the crown of life that God has promised to those who love Him." Our view changes from a "here" view to a "there" view, our eternal hope awaiting us.

Joy happens when we live in God's presence. For the child of God pursuing righteous living we can trust

God to satisfy our needs. Matthew 6:33 states, "Seek first the kingdom of God and His righteousness and all these things (food, clothing, and shelter) will be provided for you." As we allow God to reign in our lives, we can fully trust Him to satisfy our needs.

Joy comes when we spend time praising God, such as focusing on the abundant blessings around us over our grumbling, complaining, and dissatisfaction of our circumstances during trials. I Thessalonians 5:16-18 says, "Rejoice always! Pray constantly. Give thanks in everything, for this is God's will for you in Christ Jesus." As we mature and grow in our faith, we must give an outlet to our expression of praising God through rejoicing, prayer, and being thankful. This is called worship, and we are called to express our love and gratitude to the Lord in this way.

When we live in joy of our Lord, life's irritations suddenly seem insignificant. Trials take on a new purpose. Our focus becomes clear as we set our hearts on the one who shepherds our path to righteousness all the length of our days.

O'MA AND THE GIRLS

Tychicus, our dearly loved brother, faithful servant, and fellow slave in the Lord, will tell you all the news about me. I have sent him to you for this very purpose, so that you may know how we are and so that he may encourage your hearts. He is with Onesimus, a faithful and dearly loved brother, who is one of you. They will tell you about everything here. Aristarchus, my fellow prisoner, greets you, as does Mark, Barnabas's cousin (concerning whom you have received instructions: if he comes to you, welcome him), and so does Jesus who is called Justus. These alone of the circumcision are my coworkers for the kingdom of God, and they have been a comfort to me.

Colossians 4:7-11

Speaking at camp for the first time and going by myself was a little nerve wracking. For days leading up to my departure for camp, my stomach churned, and I questioned the wisdom in deciding to do this. I loved teaching boys and girls and had at one time been a part of a thriving children's ministry at my church. But it had been four years since I last taught children. On top of that, the high school and college aged counselors would be in attendance, causing my stress level to skyrocket.

I kept going to the Lord with my concerns, nervousness, anxiety, and qualms. He kept reminding me that He was with me in all the things He has called me to do. "It is in His power and strength we are able to do anything at all," a good friend rebuked me.

Finally, the day arrived, and I packed up my car and headed towards camp, praying all the while for as many things regarding the junior children's camp I could think to pray for. I arrived just in time for the staff meeting, as wary eyes darted and shifted, "checking me out" surreptitiously. I introduced myself, and I offered the staff a couple bags of chocolates and let them know that I had been praying for them, especially for this week of counseling.

Waiting for the campers to arrive, I felt awkward, not knowing what to do. Plucking up the courage, I began to go around and greet some of the female counselors. When all of a sudden, I saw a golf cart with the camp nurse I knew and her granddaughter (who I used to teach in VBS). God was bringing comfort to me through the familiarity of people who loved me!

Later, though, I began to feel slightly out of place and anxious again just before it was time for me to speak. I quoted the verse for the week and immediately felt the calming presence of the Lord. After chapel was over, a lady I had noticed earlier in the afternoon came up to me and announced, "Hi! I'm Rochelle! And this is Kate, her daughter Sarah, and Lil, but we call her O'ma. We are here volunteering in the kitchen this week."

God had brought this group of ladies to be an encouragement and comfort to me during my week at camp. They called themselves my friends and joined me at all the meals. They invited me to visit them in their cabin, even sending Kate's daughter, Sarah, to my cabin to tell me they had a gift for me. When I got to their cabin, O'ma Lil was so excited to give me a gift basket of goodies in case I got hungry during the afternoons and evenings.

As we sat there and talked, I found out how much we had in common, as wives and mothers, even as daughters. We spent a delightful afternoon chatting, laughing, and crying a little. Our hearts were being knit together in the love of Christ. All week long, they did things to encourage me as I spoke with the campers. They invited me into their circle to play games, enjoy chips and salsa, and even to wait out a tornado warning in our pajamas!

By the end of the week, I felt like I had known these ladies for years. Each one blessed my heart in a different way, encouraged me through the week, offered helpful insights and wise counsel. God directed these ladies in my life to help me in my ministry at camp. They ultimately were workers together with me in sharing the gospel with the boys and girls that week.

I didn't just have these women praying for me and encouraging me during Jr. Camp week. There were others who sent emails, texts, and phone calls to let me know that they were praying and encouraging me in this ministry. Many continued to contact me after the week was over to find out how it went, what was the outcome of "campfire confessions," and if boys and girls came to Christ. I learned quickly that ministry is not a one-person gig. It takes many people praying, working, and ministering to make the gospel of Christ come alive to a world dying to know Him.

One thing is very clear about the Apostle Paul. He was a great friend. He made friends, and he was a friend. I love that he personalized his greetings directly to individuals by name and not just a group. If you count all the people Paul mentions in his letters, there are more than 100 Christians he addresses. Wherever he was serving or imprisoned, Paul thought very fondly of his friends.

Also, in this letter to the church at Colossae and the church at Ephesus, Paul was encouraging them that he was praying for him as he was prison bound. Not only did Paul pray for his friends and the churches he was writing to, he continued to teach them about Christ. His witnessing never stopped, and he loved to hear about the burdens others had because he would send his faithful friends and co-laborers to help in different areas. Two very important friends he had during the writing of Colossians were Tychicus and Onesimus.

Tychicus was described as a "beloved brother" of Paul's. He was also Paul's fellow servant in Christ. Although not an apostle himself, he worked side by side along Paul in the service of the Lord, even when things were diffi-cult. He was also trustworthy. Paul entrusted Tychicus to carry this letter to share at the church in Colossae, and later to Crete and Ephesus. And, I imagine, it wasn't easy being a friend to Paul because of the many enemies he had. Tychicus was a loyal and true friend.

Onesimus, whose name means "one of you," had been a runaway slave, now being sent back to his owner as a new creation in Christ! But in his time with the Apostle Paul, Onesimus became a "faithful and beloved" friend. In a short time, Onesimus had become a Christ follower and fellow laborer with Paul in the ministry in Rome. Understand that Paul's condition as a prisoner could well have been difficult to handle, but he proved himself to Paul as a bond servant to the Lord.

Proclaiming the Word, sharing the Gospel, carrying the burdens of our brothers and sisters in Christ, witnessing, and praying for the church are wonderful ways we can all participate in the work here on Earth. When we have "faithful and beloved" co-laborers, the burden is lifted, and work is lighter. We encourage, support, and involve ourselves together for the sake of the Gospel of Christ. We do it together. Co-laborers in Christ.

> He told them: "The harvest is abundant,
> but the workers are few.
> Therefore, pray to the Lord of the harvest
> to send out workers into His harvest."
> Luke 10:2

GIRLFRIENDS

Dear friends, let us love one another, because love is from God and everyone who loves has been born of God and knows God. The one who does not love does not know God, because God is love. God's love was revealed among us in this way: God sent His One and Only Son into the world so that we might live through Him. Love consists in this: not that we loved God, but that He loved us and sent His Son to be the propitiation for our sins. Dear friends, if God loved us in this way, we also much love one another. No one has ever seen God. If we love one another, God remains in us and His love is perfected in us.

1 John 4:7-12

I belong to a group of unlikely friends. At first, we called ourselves "The Outsiders." We met under unlikely circumstances. We each have our own unique stories to tell, live in different socio-economic situations, have different sized families, different sized homes, different everything. And yet, brought together by helping one friend unpack dishes and move into her new house, our hearts began to form a bond of love in Christ. We are now called "The Girlfriends" when we talk about ourselves. It makes my heart smile when I think of the adventures we have shared over the last three years.

In this group of "girlfriends," we've laughed and cried, prayed and sat at the feet of Jesus in Bible study. We support each other, rejoice with each other, chastise each other and weep with each other. Our hearts continue to be knit together as we grow in the Lord and in love for one another. They are the group I reach out to when writer's block has consumed my mind, when I'm frustrated due to lack of sleep, or when I'm excited to sign a new book contract. Their inclusion of me in this group is unique and special. I don't take their friendship for granted.

I John is such a beautiful reminder that we need to value our fellowship with the Lord and other believers. So much of the world sets about to destroy and deceive followers of Christ, but the truth is that the world will know us by our love for God and one another. These verses remind me of my "girlfriends," and they aren't the only ones. God has blessed my life with many women and men, who, at different times and for different purposes, walk the journey of life with me.

God has blessed me with four wonderful sisters-in-law. They love and accept me for who I am. They pray for me, encourage me, and show me the grace and love of Jesus. Each one has played valuable roles in my walk and spiritual growth, and it is my hope and prayer that I've been equally encouraging to them in their spiritual journey.

When others, especially unbelievers, see the love we have for one another, a *phileo* (brotherly) love, God's love (*agape*) is revealed through His Son, Jesus

Christ. Our love reflects the love of our Lord. We walk this path here on Earth to be an example and shine light for those who come behind us. We shine our lights brightly when we love one another, and God remains in us and matures us to be more like His Son.

God continues to teach me His love for the world through the gift of friends. Proverbs teaches us that "a friend loves at all times," "a man that has friends must show himself friendly," "the wounds of a friend are trustworthy," and "the sweetness of a friend is better than self-counsel" (17:17; 18:24; 27:6; 27:9). When we love, our love is from God, and, as members of the family of God, we are commanded to love one another to the point of laying our lives on the line for each other (John 15:13).

Reflection

Are you a good friend? What makes you a good friend?

Can others see the love you have for your friends, family, or brothers and sisters in Christ?

What are some ways you can improve your role as a friend?

LEAVE IT BETTER THAN YOU FOUND IT

But Jesus has now obtained a superior ministry, and to that degree He is the mediator of a better covenant, which has been legally enacted on better promises.

Hebrews 8:6

Walking with my Aunt through a park, I noticed she wore an empty draw-string backpack. Too involved in our visiting, I didn't bother to ask her why she was wearing it. Then it became obvious to me as she bent down occasionally and picked up trash left behind by fellow hikers and dog walkers. Not breaking stride or conversation, she would put the trash into the backpack. When we got back to our vehicles, she emptied out her bag into the trash bin. I looked at her quizzically and she responded, "I try to leave things better than I found it."

My parents instilled this same precept in my brothers' and my life as we were growing up. When we visited someone, we picked up the toys, made the beds, hung up the towels, rinsed out the sink, and helped with the table settings and dishes after a meal. Whatever we could do to help our host, we did it. In my own home, my husband and I raised our daughters to do the same thing. We leave things better than when we found it.

After a recent trip to visit family, I wondered if we left them better than when we found them. I received my answer almost immediately as my family and I got texts and messages commenting on how much they enjoyed our visit and they can't wait to do it again. Pictures have been shared, and I observed the facial responses of our loved ones. True smiles, happy countenances, and warm embraces fill picture after picture. Leaving them better than we found them.

When Jesus came to Earth, He had a plan to fulfill. His Father's will was that Jesus had come to die for the sins of many (Hebrews 9:28). Jesus' ministry was to become the priest who would, "once and for all," make the final sacrifice, the perfect sacrifice, better than all those who came before Him. For they were not able to offer forgiveness of sin and save people from their sin, offering them eternal life. Only Christ could do this. He became a "better priest" with a "better covenant" that is founded on "better promises." Jesus was leaving us "better than how He found us."

In the Old Testament, Moses had been the mediator between God and man. The New Testament mediator is found in Jesus Christ, being now the only mediator between God and man. "For there is one God and one mediator between God and humanity, Christ Jesus, Himself human" (1 Timothy 2:5). His ministry here on Earth is "better" because it is now based on a better covenant with better promises.

The Prophet Jeremiah declared the better covenant, the new covenant, that would be forthcoming (Jeremiah 31:31-34). This better covenant was established at the cross. Jesus is now the "Mediator of the New Covenant" in Hebrews 9:15. The gospel is available to both the Jew and the Gentile, and we rejoice in the New Covenant being available to all mankind.

However, we must not negate or set aside the "Old Covenant," made up of the Law. While the New Covenant of Grace does bring freedom from the Law of Moses (Galatians 5:1), it does not bring freedom of disobedience and sin against a Holy God (Romans 8:1-4). The Law limited us, and the New Covenant through Jesus Christ sets us free. Christ, through His grace, is leaving us better than He found us.

Reflection

Do you leave people better than you found them?

How can you be "better" at leaving things better than you found them?

If you've never put your faith in the "better way" of Jesus Christ, what is keeping you from choosing the "better promise" of the "better covenant" through Him? Friend, I'm praying for you to accept the "better gift of grace" through Jesus's sacrifice, once for all.

NOTES

1. https://www.moralstories.org/frog-hot-water/#:~:text=Moral%3A%20The%20frog%20couldn't,before%20you%20need%20to%20jump.
2. Lysa Terkeurst, It's Not Supposed to be This Way (Nelson Books: A Division of Thomas Nelson, 2018), 225.
3. Warren W. Wiersbe, The Bible Exposition Commentary New Testament Volume 1 (Victor, 1989, 2001), 643.
4. https://www.quotes.net/quote/37984
5. https://hymnary.org/hymn/HSH31810/126

TOPICAL INDEX

Promises & Provisions

Trials & Suffering

Comfort & Peace

Proverbs & Precepts

BIBLIOGRAPHY

Doctor, Courtney. *Steadfast: A Devotional Bible Study on the Book of James.* The Gospel Coalition, 2019.

Holman Christian Standard Bible Study Bible. Holman Bible Publishers, 2010.

Kaminker, Mendy. "Pigs & Judaism: Deep Revulsion, But a Promising Future." 2013. https://www.chabad.org/library/article_cdo/aid/2376474/jewish/Pigs-Judaism.htm

Keller, W. Phillip. *A Shepherd Looks at Psalm 23.* Zondervan, 1970, 2007.

Terkeurst, Lysa. *It's Not Supposed to be This Way.* Nelson Books, 2018.

Walvoord, John F. and Roy B. Zuck. *The Bible Knowledge Commentary: An Exposition of the Scriptures by Dallas Seminary Faculty Old Testament.* Victor Books, 1988.

Walvoord, John F. and Roy B. Zuck. *The Bible Knowledge Commentary: An Exposition of the Scriptures by Dallas Seminary Faculty New Testament.* Victor Books, 1983.

Wiersbe, Warren W. *The Bible Exposition Commentary History.* Victor, 2003.

Wiersbe, Warren W. *The Bible Exposition Commentary New Testament*, Volume 1 & 2. Victor, 1989, 2001.

Wiersbe, Warren W. *The Bible Exposition Commentary Old Testament Pentateuch.* Victor, 2001.

Wiersbe, Warren W. *The Bible Exposition Commentary Prophets.* Victor, 2002.

Wiersbe, Warren W. *The Bible Exposition Commentary Wisdom and Poetry.* Victor, 2004.